D1321208

ÉDUCATION
N° 3

CANADIAN
GEOGRAPHICAL
EDUCATION

L'ENSEIGNEMENT
DE LA GÉOGRAPHIE
AU CANADA

Edited by / Sous la direction de

ROCH CHOQUETTE, Université de Sherbrooke
JOHN WOLFORTH, Mc Gill University
MARCIEN VILLEMURE, Université d'Ottawa

Association canadienne
des Géographes
Canadian Association
of Geographers

Éditions de l'Université
d'Ottawa
University of Ottawa
Press

1980

CANADIAN GEOGRAPHICAL EDUCATION

L'ENSEIGNEMENT DE LA GÉOGRAPHIE AU CANADA

Fabriqué au Canada
Printed and bound in Canada

Cet ouvrage a été publié grâce à une subvention du
Conseil des Arts du Canada.

This book has been published with the help of a grant
from the Canada Council

ÉDUCATION
N° 3

CANADIAN GEOGRAPHICAL EDUCATION

L'ENSEIGNEMENT DE LA GÉOGRAPHIE AU CANADA

Edited by / Sous la direction de

ROCH CHOQUETTE, Université de Sherbrooke
JOHN WOLFORTH, Mc Gill University
MARCIEN VILLEMURE, Université d'Ottawa

Association canadienne des Géographes
Canadian Association of Geographers

Éditions de l'Université d'Ottawa
University of Ottawa Press

1980

À/TO

PIERRE
DAGENAIS

NEVILLE
SCARFE

pioneers and leaders in the field of
geographic education in Canada

pionniers et maîtres à penser de la
didactique de la géographie au Canada

PRÉFACE

La Faculté d'Éducation de l'Université d'Ottawa est heureuse de s'associer au travail du comité sur l'Éducation de l'Association canadienne des géographes en publiant son recueil d'articles sur l'enseignement de la géographie tant au niveau élémentaire que secondaire et en incluant ce recueil dans sa collection *Éducation*.

La réalisation de cette publication a été facilitée par la collaboration des Éditions de l'Université d'Ottawa.

Nous espérons que l'accueil réservé à ce volume par les professeurs de géographie œuvrant à tous les niveaux d'enseignement, par les didacticiens et leurs étudiants viendra corroborer le bien fondé de notre présomption première.

The Faculty of Education of the University of Ottawa is pleased to contribute to the work of the Education Committee of the Canadian Association of Geographers by publishing its selection of articles on the teaching of geography at both elementary and secondary levels and by including this selection in its *Education* collection.

The realization of this publication was made possible by the cooperation of the University of Ottawa Press.

It is hoped that the reception reserved for this volume by geography teachers at all instruction levels, by geography teachers in teacher training institutions as well as their students, will corroborate the merit of our basic presumption.

Yves POIRIER,
Doyen/Dean

TABLE DES MATIÈRES
TABLE OF CONTENTS

Préface ix
Avant-propos / Forword xiii

LE CONTENU/THE CONTENT

1. School Geography in Canada: an Historical Perspective .. 3
   GEORGE TOMKINS,
   University of British Columbia
2. Curriculum, Geography and the Canadian Context 19
   F. GEOFFREY JONES,
   Memorial University of Newfoundland
3. Teaching Geography in the Elementary School 45
   YVAN CASSIDY,
   Acadia University
4. Geography and the Environment 59
   JOHN TOWLER,
   Renison College, University of Waterloo

L'APPRENANT/THE LEARNER

5. Mapping in the Early Years of Schooling............... 71
   DENNIS MILBURN,
   University of British Columbia
6. Environmental Perception 89
   K.G. DUECK,
   University of Calgary
7. Le problème du vocabulaire dans l'enseignement de la
   géographie 99
   RÉAL GUAY,
   Université Laval
8. The Longitudinal Aspect of Evaluation in Geography 115
   GERALD T. RIMMINGTON,
   Mount Allison University

L'ENSEIGNANT/THE TEACHER

9. Fondements théoriques de la géographie et applications
   pédagogiques 125
   ROCH CHOQUETTE,
   Université de Sherbrooke
10. Réflexions sur l'enseignement de la géographie urbaine
    au secondaire 143
    MARCIEN VILLEMURE,
    Université d'Ottawa

11. Hiérarchie d'apprentissage et structuration d'un contenu
à enseigner en géographie 151
MONIQUE LAPOINTE AUBIN,
Ministère de l'Éducation,
Province de Québec.

12. Research in Geographical Education 165
JOHN WOLFORTH
Mc Gill University

AVANT-PROPOS/FOREWORD

It is a great pleasure to introduce this set of essays on geogographical education. Whilst geography has in recent times a subject of great importance in most parts of Canada, both at school and at university, no vigorous discourse has yet developed on the nature of education in this important area of the school curriculum. This volume will perhaps go someway towards remedying this condition and towards initiating lively discussions on the various aspects of the field dealt with by its contributors.

When the possibility of putting together this volume was first mooted, it was decided not to be prescriptive, but rather to ask potential authors to contribute an essay on one aspect of the field which they found interesting, or in which they were currently doing research. To the delighted surprise of the editors, the essays which were subsequently submitted seemed to fall into a coherent structure and to deal in their separate ways with distinctive areas of interest. In addition they attested to the tremendous vigour of geographical education in Canada, a vigour not always apparent to its practitioners each working within the confines of his/her own provincial constraints.

In spite of this potential insularity, moroever, the realization arose that we are by and large subject to many of the same influences, and share a common developmental tradition and concern. Perhaps remarkably, whether francophone or anglophone, whether from British Columbia or Nova Scotia, we seemed to share many of the same points of reference and to reflect a view of geographical education discernibly different from that found in, say, the United States, Britain, France, or Germany. What remains is to refine this distinctively Canadian view and to identify the contribution which we may be able to make to its future development.

L'acte d'enseigner s'appuie évidemment sur la maîtrise d'une matière. Mais d'une façon particulière pour l'enseignement élémentaire et secondaire, cette maîtrise de la discipline doit s'adapter aux principales caractéristiques intellectuelles de l'étudiant selon les divers stages de son âge mental. Les deux considérants précédents, maîtrise de la discipline et spécificités intellectuelles de l'étudiant, ont un sens par rapport à l'acte d'enseigner dans la mesure où ils s'insèrent dans un cadre de communication pédagogique.

L'objet de ce livre est de donner aux professeurs de géographie l'occasion d'explorer ces trois sphères de connaissances reliées intrinsèquement à l'enseignement de leur matière. À partir d'articles rédigés par des universitaires canadiens spécialisés dans l'étude de l'enseignement de la géographie à l'élémentaire et au secondaire, on examinera successivement la matière à enseigner à travers les programmes passés et récents et les exigences intellectuelles spécifiques aux divers niveaux d'âge. Enfin on offrira des suggestions méthodologiques pouvant permettre un cadre pédagogique plus efficace.

Ce recueil, nous l'espérons, permettra aux enseignants et aux chercheurs de mieux cerner les composantes de l'acte d'enseigner, et ainsi accéder à un niveau supérieur d'efficacité et de satisfaction.

JOHN WOLFORTH,
Mc Gill University

ROCH CHOQUETTE,
Université de Sherbrooke

LE CONTENU
THE CONTENT

SCHOOL GEOGRAPHY IN CANADA:
AN HISTORICAL PERSPECTIVE

GEORGE TOMKINS
University of British Columbia

Geography teaching in Canada began with instruction in the elements of the subject taugh by the Jesuits in New France as part of mathematics and natural philosophy. Later, schools for teaching the practical arts were established during the 1660's by Bishop Laval at St. Joachim and Quebec. These practical arts included agriculture and navigation, two subjects of obvious importance in the fledgling colony. According to L.-E. Hamelin, aspects of geography (hydrography, surveying, catography and mathematical geography) were taught in connection with these studies. He regards this first long phase of geography in French Canada as extending to 1830. The latter part of this phase was featured by the publication in 1804 of the first Canadian geography textbook.[1]

The second phase of French-Canadian geography extended from 1830 to 1880. In 1835, the teaching of geography was formally recommended in the primary and secondary schools of Lower Canada (Quebec). A year later, the normal school in Montreal began to instruct prospective teachers of the subject. Shortly thereafter, the Brothers of the Christian Schools arrived in Montreal and began to supply manuals for geography courses in the schools of the city. Yet geography had not yet attained fully autonomy and most of it was taught in conjunction with arithmetic, sacred history and geology.

Hamelin dates the third phase of French-Canadian geography from 1880. Three years earlier, the oldest geographical society in Canada had been founded at Quebec. This society published a bulletin which appeared from 1880 to 1934. Quebec contributed to the delegation which unofficially represented Canada at the International Geographical Congress held in Venice in 1881. The third phase of

---

[1] This discussion of the development of French-Canadian geography is based on Louis-Edmond HAMELIN, "Petite histoire de géographie dans le Québec et à l'Université Laval", *Cahiers de géographie de Quebec*, VII (October 1962-March 1963), pp. 1-16; "Bibliographie non-annotée concernant la pénétration de la géographie dans le Québec", *Notes et Documents*, II, *Travaux de l'Institut de géographie de l'Université Laval* (Québec: Laval University, 1960), pp. 8-46; "Bibliographie non-annotée concernant la pénétration de la géographie dans le Québec", *Cahiers de géographie de Québec*, VII (April-September 1960), pp. 345-359. See also G. S. TOMKINS, "Griffith Taylor and Canadian Geography", Ph.D., thesis, University of Washington, 1967. pp. 138-144.

French-Canadian geography closed in 1910 with the establishment of a chair (though not a department as such) at the School of Higher Commercial Studies, a division of the University of Montreal. This professorship was held by Henri Laureys from Belgium and marked the emergence of economic and commercial geography in the school and college curricula of Quebec. Significantly, these aspects of geography were also receiving the first serious attention in English-speaking Canada and in the United States at this time. Later, in 1914, Professor Laureys published his *Essai de géographie du Canada* in Brussels and introduced it, along with several other Belgian textbooks, to schools and colleges in Quebec.

Early school geography in English Canada as in French Canada was slow to emerge as a separate subject and was often taught in association with religious and biblical studies in a period when moral education in the sense of indoctrination was emphasized. Geography thus frequently began with the study of ancient, i.e. biblical lands. At the university level, the first appearance of geography in the curriculum seems to have occurred at the University of New Brunswich in 1800. The course covered the general field of earth or physical science and thus anticipated the later development of the subject. It was short-lived, however, and after its demise university geography in Canada was almost non-existent throughout the nineteenth century. It thus had to be developed as a school subject without significant academic support, a condition that would obtain until our own time.[2]

In the absence of their own texts, teachers and pupils in the early schools of English Canada were perforce required to rely on American books. Teachers themselves were frenquently American and in Upper Canada (Ontario) the fear was expressed as early as 1799 that such itinerants "tinctured the minds of their pupils with their own political views." If anything, American textbooks were even more feared than teachers so that for a time they were officially banned from use; teachers were required to be British-born or to be naturalized British subjects. There was particular objection to books that, among other subversive influences, included "geographies setting forth (American cities) as the largest and finest in the world..." Such geographies included those of the famous Yale divine, Jedidiah Morse, who became the most successful post-revolutionary author of American geography textbooks.[3] In 1847 one of these was in use in 651 schools in Upper Canada and two years later it received the official sanction of the General Board of Education.

---

[2] For references to the early development of geography, particularly school geography in English-speaking Canada see TOMKINS, *op. cit.*, pp. 144-164 and E. J. QUICK, "The Development of Geography and History Curricula in the Elementary Schools of Ontario, 1946-1966", Ed. D. thesis, University of Toronto, 1967.

[3] R. H. BROWN, "The American Geographies of Jedidiah Morse", *Annals of the Association of American Geographers*, 31 (September, 1941), pp. 145-217.

Besides concern about the republican anti-monarchical bias of American textbooks, there was also concern about their scanty treatment of Canada. Thus one edition of Morse's books was in due course replaced by textbooks from Ireland. One of the first of these was *Geography Generalized* by Robert Sullivan. This included sections on mathematical, physical and political geography along with a short section on teaching methods. There was a lack of maps, diagrams or other illustrations and a plethora of encyclopedic information on the sizes of cities, lakes and rivers. The Irish Historical Readers were also introduced into Upper Canada and by 1860 probably served as the chief source of information for the majority of pupils in the province. Descriptive geographic outlines of the major continents were provided in story form. However, Irish texts were no more suitable for Canadian use than American texts and, if anything, devoted even less attention to Canada. For this and other reasons George Brown vigorously opposed them. In due course, the Irish Readers and American textbooks were adapted for Canadian use, a process of "Canadianization" of foreign geography and other textbooks that has continued to our own day.

Meanwhile, in 1857, one of the first native geography texts made its appearance in Upper Canada. This was J. G. Hodgins' *Geography and History of British North America*, a text designed to remedy the "scanty knowledge of their own and sister provinces" found in foreign textbooks.[4] Its publication was a tacit recognition by educators of the need to study Canada from a broad perspective. The national emphasis was explicit as Hodgins, probably anticipating Confederation, noted that "commercial intercourse has been frequent between (the colonies) and a political and social bond of sympathy has been created which renders absolutely necessary a fuller acquaintance with the mutual history, conditions and capabilities of each." From henceforth, textbooks were expected to promote "national ideas" but such ideas were definitely to be pro-British and Christian. Books such as Hodgins' reflected a recognition that history and geography should complement each other. They were in fact to be called "sister studies" for "If we are to know everything about a country we must study both..." In this concept lay the seed of the modern idea of social studies as a unified study.

Concepts of geography teaching that were prevalent in nineteenth century American school geography, as described by Dryer in 1924, seem also to have existed in Canada.[5] This is suggested by books teaching physical geography that emphasized "the striking proof of Divine skill and omnipotence." Dryer, in referring to a similar providential view of geography found in the United States refers to "the attention given to religion and curiosities." He called this the

4 QUICK, *op. cit.*, p. 39.
5 R. DRYER, "A Century of Geographic Education in the United States", *Annals of the Association of American Geographers*, XIV (September 1924), pp. 117-149.

"Wonder Book" stage of geography which superseded without fully replacing an earlier Gazeteer stage—the latter based on a catechetical question and answer mode of teaching derived from biblical instruction. In the "Wonder Book" stage, unusual, interesting and spectacular phenomena were emphasized, e.g., volcanoes, geysers and "remarkable races and animals of mankind." Even as geography became more scientific, the "good-God-in-nature" theme (as Dryer aptly termed it) remained prominent. This was evident in the textbooks written by the most prominent scientific geographer of the mid-century in the United States, Professor Arnold Guyot of Princeton. Some of his books were later used in Canada. His environmentalist philosophy was indicated by placing the geography of nature before the geography of man because the latter "is regulated by the former."

Guyot's work marked the appearance of what Dryer has termed the "Natural Teleology" stage in nineteenth century school geography. The subject became more scientific as the work of Humboldt and Agassiz entered the textbooks. The first isothermal maps and profiles appeared. This stage established the tradition that "physical geography deals only with the remote and has nothing to do with the familiar land and sky at home." The Natural Teleology stage was followed by those of General Physiography and Specialized Physiography. These stages were based on the work of Darwin and Huxley as interpreted by William Morris Davis, R. A. Tarr and others. Davis taught at Harvard and by the turn of the century was recognized as one of the two or three leading world geographers. *Tarr's Elementary Physical Geography*, published in 1895, became a standard textbook which was based on geomorphology and Davis' cycle of erosion theory. Geography became a laboratory subject at this time. Tarr's book was shortly introduced into Ontario and British Columbia.

The catechetical and moralistic approach to geography teaching used during much of the nineteenth century is illustrated by the following as quoted by Quick from Hodgins' *Easy Lessons in General Geography* :

Q :   Are all nations equally civilized ?
A :   No, some are uncivilized, others are half-civilized.
Q :   How do nations become fully civilized ?
A :   By means of the religion of the Bible, aided by education.

Hodgins defined geography as "a description of the Earth, of its peoples and products..." His providential view of the subject was illustrated by this explanation of the Earth's origins :

Q :   Who made the Earth ?
A :   "In the beginning God created the heaven and the earth."

Further clues to the nature and content of school geography are clear from examination questions such as these set for Toronto elementary school pupils in the 1860's :

1. What are the boundaries of Canada?
2. Name the islands and lakes of South America.
3. Mention the principal rivers of France and the towns situated upon any of them.

Uniform textbooks and examinations of this kind based upon them became a method of standardizing the geography curriculum.

The desire for order and system led to a methodology of teaching based on such devices as a "Formula for Describing a State or Country", an approach reminiscent of the labelling system ("Relief, Surface, Soils, Climate, Vegetation", etc.) used in our own day by geography teachers as categories for regional description. Nevertheless, such questions as "Why do the days become warmer as they grow longer?" illustrated a real effort to go beyond a conception of geography as a memoriter subject. A good deal of emphasis was placed on map reading, drawing and sketching skills. All of these efforts represented a desire to overcome the major criticism that geography was a mistaught subject "because pupils are taught words and not things..." The most enlightened geography teachers advocated principles as progressive as any advocated today. The importance of local studies as a prelude to more general studies was understood together with the concomitant principles of proceeding from the "known to the unknown" and from the concrete to the abstract in an inducative fashion.

The famous Ontario School Act of 1871 crowned Egerton Ryerson's efforts to establish a free, compulsory, centralized and uniform system of elementary education. It provided a curriculum pattern that would remain relatively unchanged until the 1930's. The programme of studies embodied as one major objective that of providing "some knowledge of Geography and History, of the Civil Government and Institutions of our own country, and, in all cases, of the first principles of Christian morals, as essential to every honest man and good citizen." Promotion from one class to another required in geography a demonstration of very precise knowledge stated in terms reminiscent of our modern behavioural objectives. Thus, the pupil was expected

To be able to point out on a map of the World each Continent and Ocean and to know which part of the map is North, South, East or West.
To know the names and uses of the principal lines drawn on the map of the World, such as Meridians, Equator, Parallels of Latitude, Tropics, Arctic and Antarctic Circles.

The school system developed by Ryerson for Ontario became the prototype for systems in the new western provinces after Confederation. British Columbia's first superintendent of education, John Jessop had, in fact, been a student of Ryerson. In many ways, the growth of geography in the westernmost province, replicated what had occurred in Ontario.[6] Thus, the Irish National Readers were used

---

[6] W. E. TOPPING, "The Historical Development of the Teaching of Geography in British Columbia", M. A. thesis, University of British Columbia, 1963.

during the colonial period, i.e., before 1871. After that year, Ontario textbooks came into use, some of which, irrelevantly enough, required west coast pupils to memorize the county names and boundaries of that province. An exception was Pillan's *Ancient Geography*, published in Edinburgh and used in the province's first high school, opened at Victoria in 1876. The book reflected a widespread view that the study of geography should assist the study of classical literature. It was used in conjunction with primers of physical geography, physiography, geology, astronomy and botany. Geography was a popular subject in British Columbia for, Topping tells us, in 1879 the number of pupils studying it was very much higher than the number studying history.

As noted earlier, Tarr's famous physical geography text came into use in Ontario and British Columbia before 1900. This descriptive physical treatment of the subject was known as the "New Geography." Shortly, as also noted earlier, more economic and commercial (or industrial) geography would be introduced into both provinces.

I. — THE STATUS OF GEOGRAPHY AND GEOGRAPHY TEACHING IN CANADA, 1900-1945

The emergence of physical and economic geography as two separate and unrelated strands of the subject reflected major developments in the school curriculum of the United States at the turn of the century. Clearly, these trends were not without influence in Canada. Physical geography south of the border, often called earth science, eventually became absorbed into general science. Economic geography sometimes came to be absorbed as "human geography" into history or social studies.

The trends described arose out of the work of the famous Committee of Ten which in the 1890's reorganized and differentiated the high school curriculum, creating a multiple track as opposed to the prevailing single track academic curriculum. The Committee organized several "conferences", i.e. sub-committees, one of which dealt with geography.[7] In fact, despite the longstanding recognition of the subject, more dissatisfaction was expressed regarding it than was expressed for any other subject. The nine members, who included William Morris Davis, advanced a view of geography radically different from any then found in school curricula. The subject was defined as a study of "the physical environment of man", drawing its subject matter from a half dozen natural sciences.

Such was the prestige of the conference group and of the Committee of Ten that within a decade physical geography was estab-

        7   W. D. PATTISON, "Geography in the High School", *Annals of the Association of American Geographers*, LII (September, 1962), pp. 280-284. See also Sidney ROSEN, "A Short History of High School Geography to 1936", *The Journal of Geography*, LVI (December, 1957), pp. 405-412.

lished strongly in American high schools and was accepted as a college entrance subject by the College Entrance Examination Board. Its popularity, however, was shortlived, due in part to the lack of trained teachers and to the complete neglect of human geography. In time, as noted above, it was absorbed into general science. This trend was already evident in British Columbia by 1909. By 1921 in that province, physical geography had disappeared from the curriculum as a separate subject. In Ontario, it retained its hold much longer and came to be based on a textbook, *Ontario High School Physical Geography* that ran through several editions and was used by several generations of students there and in other Canadian provinces. In 1937, it finally disappeared as teachers were told that "while physical geography is the basis of all geography, only those aspects of it which directly affect human activities need be included in the course."[8]

In the United States, economic geography began as an attempt to "humanize" physical geography. By 1910, as commercial geography, it was fairly well established in the high school curriculum. In response to what was seen as the Committee of Ten's overemphasis on physical geography, it was urged that pupils learn "how the history of nations has been shaped by geographic conditions" and "appreciate the responses which human life everywhere makes to its physical surroundings." Mark Jefferson and R. H. Whitheck were among the prominent geographers on the National Education Association committee that proposed a course along these lines in 1909.[9] Although economic geography gained something of a foothold in the American high school curriculum, by the 1930's it was at a low ebb. In part this reflected the rise of the social studies; equally it reflected the effort of the Committee of Ten to streamline the high school curriculum by relegating everything but pure physical geography to the elementary level. There it would remain throughout the United States and much of Canada for many years.

In Ontario by 1914, the first year of the high school programme included a required course entitled Commercial and Map Geography. This emphasized the study of Ontario, Canada and the British Empire but seventeen foreign countries were also studied with emphasis on:

> ... their principal resources, industries and productions; chief centres of population; condition of the people and their forms of government; the influence of their geographical conditions on their political, industrial and commercial development.

The best known texts produced for this and other similar courses was a series edited by Professor George W. Cornish of The Ontario College of Education, University of Toronto. These texts

---

[8] A. T. CARNAHAN, "Background Material for the Past Fifty Years in Secondary School Geography" (London, Ontario: Canadian Association of Geographers, 1964), 12 pp. (mimeographed).

[9] T. F. CHAMBERLAIN, "Report of the Committee on Secondary School Geography", *Journal of Geography*, VIII (September, 1909), pp. 1-9.

provided a systematic or topical treatment of commercial geography by commodities. Commerce and transportation were also treated. A concession to regional geography was made in the form of an overview of the countries of the British Empire. This included standard imperialistic sentiments of the day reflecting a jingoism that Canadians have usually ascribed to American textbooks. London was described as a great city due to "the industry, the thrift... the sterling business ability... (and) the honest dealing of its people." It was averred that India had "wonderfully improved" under British rule. Although the book was written and published in Canada, Canadian pupils in the several provinces in which the series was authorized found France described in one volume as "our neighbour across the channel."[10]

The genesis of the social studies movement can be found in ideas of correlation of subjects derived from the German philosopher Herbart whose disciples in Germany and North America began to apply them in the 1890's as a basis for curriculum reform more than half a century after their master's death. By 1905, these ideas were so well established in Ontario that Quick marks that year as the start of an era in education that would span three decades. The Herbartian famous Five Form Steps of teaching: Preparation, Presentation, Comparison, Generalization and Application became the basis of teacher training and, as set out in geography, history and social studies manuals provided a uniform method that Phillips claims influenced Canadian schools from coast to coast.[11]

In the United States, the social studies movement is often formally dated from 1916 with the publication of the report entitled *The Social Studies in Secondary Education*. The most significant recommendation of this report was that work be organized not "on the basis of the formal social sciences but on the basis of concrete problems of vital importance to society and of immediate interest to the pupil." This marked the emergence of "citizenship" as an explicit concern of the social studies, along with further efforts to correlate, integrate or "fuse" the disciplines. The steadily deteriorating position of geography was revealed by the recommendation that it be taught "incidentally to and as a factor in the history."[12]

In Canada, the social studies had its chief effect in the western provinces where it was being accepted into the curriculum by the end of World War I. However, especially at the secondary level and most notably in British Columbia it later came to be an "umbrella term" to refer to discrete courses in the disciplines, including geography. Al-

[10] G. W. Cornish, *Canadian Geography for Juniors*, British Columbia edition (Toronto: J. M. Dent and Sons, 1937), p. 209.

[11] C. E. Phillips, *The Development of Education in Canada* (Toronto: W. J. Gage Limited, 1957), p. 419.

[12] Rolla M. Tryon, *The Social Sciences as School Subjects* (New York: Charles Scribner's Sons, 1935), p. 17.

berta probably went farthest in integrating subject matter, in making "citizenship" attributes explicit and in utilizing such devices as projects and objective texts. After 1920, high school geography, as in the United States, went into eclipse in all the western provinces although it did retain a strong position in the elementary grades. Its status was no higher in the Maritime Provinces. Only in Quebec and Ontario was the subject at all seriously recognized.

These gloomy conclusions are confirmed by reading a useful survey of the position of geography in Canada at the time that was made by a British geographer in 1921.[13] A. D. Chapman had been a member of a committee which McGill University had established to survey geography textbooks in Canadian schools. There were seventeen textbooks authorized for use by the nine provinces. Eight of these were written in French, mostly by priests untrained in the subject. Some of those written in English were no better, containing very little physical geography, poor maps, catalogues of often incorrect facts and little or no attempt at explanation. Chapman deplored the fact that because each province was a law unto itself exchanges of teachers and textbooks were discouraged; he equally deplored provincial demands for special editions of books to meet particular provinces' imagined needs. The root of the problem was the lack of acceptance of geography as a university discipline. This lack was part of a vicious circle. At a time when university entrance requirements dominated school curricula, the non-acceptance of geography as a matriculation subject meant that schools had no incentive to offer the subject; its lack at the university level meant that trained teachers were unavailable to teach it in any event.

This situation and the high tide of social studies in nearly all provinces between the wars adequately explains the slow growth of school geography. At the university level, to be sure, some progress was made. In Quebec after 1910, during what Hamelin characterizes as a fifth stage in French-Canadian geography (lasting until 1945) the Faculty of Social Sciences at the University of Montreal appointed a French-trained professor, Emile Miller, in 1921. Hamelin regards Miller's *Terres et Peuples du Canada* as a pioneer textbook. During the period 1925-27, Jean Brunhes, one of the greatest French geographers, lectured at Montreal. At this time, two young scholars, Raymond Tanghe and Benoit Brouillette (the latter to be prominent later in UNESCO and the International Geographical Union) were doing graduate work in French leading to the first doctorates ever earned by Canadian geographers. They were later appointed to the Montreal faculty. In 1927, the noted French geographer, Raoul Blanchard, paid the first of several annual visits he would make to Canada before 1939. Blanchard did field work and taught a formal course at the University of Montreal in 1933. Thus, prior to World War II, geography

[13] A. D. CHAPMAN, "The Position of Geography in Canada", *The Geographical Teacher*, XI (Spring, 1921), pp. 52-54.

was well established in Quebec's largest university, although no graduate work was offered. It became established at Laval in 1941. The establishment of formal departments in both Quebec universities would not occur until after 1945.

In modern English-speaking Canada, Toronto would become the fountainhead of university geography. George M. Wrong, an historian, has been credited with stimulating some interest in the subject as early as 1895. This appears to have been via economic history and seems to have taken the form of commercial geography and the geography of transportation. An examination of the university calendar for the period also indicates that at least six courses in the Department of Political Economy, including cartography and physiography were relevant to geography. Thus, there was established a tradition that related geography to the social sciences on the one hand and to the natural sciences on the other. The social science bias was strengthened later as the Department of Political Economy began to offer courses that could be considered geographic. The 1919-20 university calendar listed a first year course officially labelled "Economic Geography."[14]

In that year, a young man of twenty-six, Harold Adams Innis, fresh from completing his Ph.D. at the University of Chicago, was appointed a lecturer in the Department of Political Economy at Toronto. Destined to become the dean of Canadian social scientists, Innis had a keen interest in geography that lead to his attendance at the International Geographical Congress in Cambridge in 1928. Later that year his title was changed to Assistant Professor of Economic Geography. His courses would introduce Canadian students to the work of such eminent geographers as Marion Newbigin, J. Russell Smith, V. C. Finch, O. E. Baker and Ellsworth Huntington. But Innis' appointment was only a temporary measure pending the appointment of a regular professor and the establishment of an official department at Toronto. This was accomplished in 1935, largely through Innis' efforts, with the appointment of Griffith Taylor whose arrival from Chicago (whence he had come from Australia in 1929) can be regarded as the true beginning of formal university geography in English-speaking Canada.

During the interwar period, geography was taught at a few other universities. The University of British Columbia had given the discipline partial departmental status as part of the department of geology and geography in 1922. In 1938, a geography lectureship was established at the University of Western Ontario. This was filled by Dr. Edward G. Pleva an American-trained geographer from the University of Minnesota who would in time become a prime mover of school geography in Ontario. McMaster University established a lectureship in 1939 which was filled by Dr. J. Wreford Watson who in

---

[14] TOMKINS, *op. cit.*, p. 171. This is cited from a general discussion of the development of university geography by Tomkins, pp. 169-177.

1942 become head of the second department, after Toronto, to be established in English-speaking Canada. Watson later became head of the Federal Government's Geographical Branch and thereby was able indirectly to promote the course of geography in education. In 1945, a department was established at McGill University under the chairmanship of Dr. G. H. T. Kimble.

II.—CANADIAN GEOGRAPHY TEACHING SINCE 1945

Despite the developments noted, Canadian school geography grew but slowly during the wartime and immediate post-war periods. In his 1951 survey of the status of geography in Canadian universities, Dr. Dudly Stamp the eminent British geographer made scathing references to the subject in schools that were reminiscent of the obloquy of Chapman thirty years earlier. Like his predecessor, Stamp related its low status in schools to its lack of acceptance in the universities. In the schools, the rigid prescribed curricula produced a "safe mediocrity." Lacking trained teachers, a "capes and bays" geography was dominant in a social studies context that inhibited any proper development of the subject.[15] Nevertheless, the period was one of almost unnoticed gestation for geography at all levels. The Canadian Association of Geographers was formed in 1950 with Griffith Taylor and Raoul Blanchard as its first honorary presidents. Geography was recognized in a separate methods course for teachers taught by W.E. Sager at the Ontario College of Education, an event that foreshadowed the remarkable development of the subject in the schools of that province over the next fifteen years. In 1951, geography gained a foothold in the Prairie Provinces when it achieved departmental status at the University of Manitoba. At the same institution, Professor N. V. Scarfe's appointment as Dean of Education brought to Canada in the same year the leading world figure in geographic education, a disciple of James Fairgrieve who had pioneered the teaching of the subject in Great Britain. In 1950, Scarfe had coordinated a notable international symposium under the sponsorship of UNESCO which, held in Montreal, introduced some Canadian geographers to new ideas for teaching the subject in schools.[16]

In 1952, Scarfe became chairman of the I. G. U. Commission on the Teaching of Geography. The Commission investigated the status of the subject in various countries, including Canada.[17] In the western

[15] L. D. STAMP, *Geography in Canadian Universities: A Report to the Canadian Social Science Research Council*, (Ottawa: The Council, 1951), pp. 21-25.
[16] N. V. SCARFE, *A Handbook of Suggestions on the Teaching of Geography* (Utrecht: UNESCO, 1951).
[17] INTERNATIONAL GEOGRAPHICAL UNION, *Report of the Commission on the Teaching of Geography in Schools* (Chicago: Denoyer Geppert, 1956). See also N. V. SCARFE, "The Teaching of Geography in Canada", *The Canadian Geographer*, V (1955), pp. 1-8. For the situation a few years later see John J. NEARING, "Geography in Canadian High Schools: An Emerging Trend in Social Studies", *Education* V (19), (Toronto: W. G. Gage Limited, 1964).

provinces it was "usually taught inadequately as a minor portion of social studies." In eastern Canada, geography had more status as a separate subject and had a more definite "physical basis" than that taught in the West. Too many teachers, Scarfe thought, saw geography as a handmaiden of history. A view of human geography stressing how people lived in various regions of the world belied the rhetoric of teachers that the subject should correlate physical and cultural factors. Even at the university level, the Commission found much "pseudo-scientific verbalism" and an overemphasis on generalization unsupported by detailed knowledge. As a result, geography suffered from unreality.

In 1951, Griffith Taylor retired after sixteen years in the chairmanship at Toronto. Throughout a long career on two continents he had fought valiantly for the status of geography in schools, university and community. His consistent purpose, albeit with strong environmentalist overtones, had been to promote the primary aim of all education, i.e. "to fit the child to cope adequately with the problems confronting him when he leaves school." Yet as he retired, he felt that "In my most sincere effort, I feel that I have failed, for after sixteen years of pleading, I can see no signs of any change of status for geography in the schools of Ontario." Yet he was wrong. The re-emergence of geography and history at the high school level in Ontario and the decline of the social studies had already begun. A few years earlier, Taylor had cooperated with Professor G. H. T. Kimble in the preparation of a brief to the Ontario Royal (Hope) Commission in Education. The brief reviewed the low status of geography in Canada although it conceded diplomatically that in Ontario its position was somewhat higher than that elsewhere. The usefulness of geography in military and commercial life was stressed, along with its value as part of general education, especially as an integrating or liaison subject. The brief concluded with a number of recommendations : that geography be made a matriculation subject; that it cease to be taught under the "social studies" label; that trained geography teachers be given more opportunity to promote their subject; that geography curriculae be modernized and be made more practical; that special geography rooms be established; that unqualified teachers be encouraged to attend summer schools.

Within a few years after Taylor's retirement, all these recommendations had been implemented with the result that it is safe to assert today that geography enjoys a higher status in Ontario than in any other school system in North America. This point was highlighted in 1975 when the National Council for Geographic Education held its first meeting outside the United States, in Toronto. This largest meeting in the organization's history drew the majority of its participants from Ontario, underscoring the fact that the province had the largest number of highly trained teachers of any jurisdiction on the contintent.

It would be facile to credit too much of this progress to Griffith Taylor or, indeed, to the acceptance of geography as a university discipline. However, the practical emphasis and the place of fieldwork in Ontario geography teaching at all levels may owe something to Taylor. Above all, his influence may have been personal, illustrated by the several thousand of his ex-students teaching to this day in schools and colleges in Ontario and in other provinces and countries. In Pleva's view, cited earlier, the major credit for the growth of geography in Ontario should be assigned to key people in the provincial educational system who developed programes for training specialist teachers, devised the geography syllabi and arranged for the recognition of geography as a university subject. Although some observers ascribed considerable British influence to developments in Ontario, Pleva thought otherwise :

> I believe Ontario geography is the product of Ontario. It is very much an independent mutation and is, therefore, significant. Foreign geographers may have added something but certainly the Ontario system is now self-perpetuating... Ontario geography is based, naturally, on British ideas but also on American, German, French and Russian ideas...[18]

By the late fifties or mid-sixties, geography was well established in the universities of all the western provinces. By the early seventies it was accepted in school curricula in the same provinces as social studies experienced the same decline noted earlier in Ontario. During the same period, it finally achieved a breakthrough in the Atlantic provinces as geography departments were established in Mount Allison (New Brunswick) and St. Mary's (Nova Scotia) universities, taking their place with Memorial University (Newfoundland) established earlier. School geography in these provinces grew significantly and was able to profit from the advances made earlier elsewhere, particularly in teaching methods and materials. Geography in Canada and the United States was a major beneficiary of the curriculum reform movement that took place in the early 1960's. This movement heralded a trend towards a more subject-centred regime but using the inquiry-oriented methods and "discovery" materials that had featured some social studies curricula in the earlier more child-centred era of "progressive" education.

In this "structural" revolution, which emphasized the acquisition by children of a knowledge of the structure and characteristic inquiry modes of each discipline, Canadian geography teachers were in the vanguard. In this case, British influence may have been significant. The ideas of James Fairgrieve which, though dating back to the 1920's, were consistent with the new approaches, had been brought to Canada by Scarfe and others. Fairgrieve's school textbooks exemplified teaching methods in which the pupil could undertake vicarious field study (complemented by actual fieldwork) using inductively a

---

[18]   Personal communication from Dr. E. G. Pleva, June 15, 1965.

rich variety of materials integrated with the written text and requiring active investigation by the pupil.[19] It would be a British geographer, Honeybone, another disciple of Fairgrieve, who would with his colleagues, Roberson and Long, render their mentor's ideas in modern form in a series of textbooks most of which were soon introduced to Canadian schools and adapted for Canadian use. Very shortly, indigenous Canadian texts of a similar kind would be produced by Tomkins, Weir and others.[20]

The "new" geography in school thus came, in characteristic fashion, to be spread most effectively by textbooks. Since 1960, it has reflected in a conservative fashion trends within the research discipline itself. At that level, the "new" geography on the human side has been characterized by the "quantitative revolution", by model building and by other sophisticated social science concepts and techniques. On the physical side, too, geography has become more scientific than before. In a word, it has been the systematic side that has flourished at the expense, some would say, of the regional tradition. In the United States, new approaches to school geography became symbolized by the High School Geography Project, the most notable effort in more than half a century to update the subject in that country. The project undoubtedly had an impact in Canada although as yet this has not been documented. In any event, the circumstances in the two countries were markedly different: whereas the Project in the United States was an effort to re-establish a school subject that had gone into almost total eclipse at the secondary level, in Canada such eclipse had never been as complete. Moreover, the revival of the subject in Canadian schools preceded the High School Geography Project and was, as noted above, assisted by the British influence. As a result, the relatively high status of their subject has made Canadian teachers the envy of their American colleagues. It was noteworthy that two Canadians, Angus Gunn of the University of British Columbia and Ronald Carswell of the University of Calgary were appointed to the staff of the High School Geography Project. They and other Canadians were active in the National Council for Geographic Education and Dean Neville Scarfe became in 1974-75 the first Canadian to head that body.

By 1978, a more expansive view of the subject was manifested not only in new techniques and methods but in the growth of new fields such as urban and cultural geography. These complemented rather than replaced descriptive regional geography and the traditional systematic "elements" course which had stressed, some said

19   James FAIRGRIEVE, *Geography in School* (London: University of London Press, 1926).
20   See for example A. R. GRIME, *Landscapes of the World* (Toronto: Ballhaven House Limited, 1966), adapted from R. C. HONEYBONE et al *World Geography* (London: Heinemann Educational Books Limited, 1963) and G. S. TOMKINS, T. R. WEIR et al., *A Regional Geography of North America*, 2 nd. edition (Toronto: Gage Educational Publishing, 1970).

overstressed, physical geography. Geographers played a prominent part in the burgeoning Canadian Studies movement of the 1970's. This movement could be said to have begun with Hodgetts' famous investigation of the teaching of history and civics, published in 1968 under the title *What Culture? What Heritage?* Some geography teachers argued that the ignorance of Canada by students as revealed in Hodgetts' findings might have been less apparent had he included geography in his survey for by then the study of their own country was staple fare in geography classrooms. It was possibly significant that Hodgets reported "a feeling for the land"—a geographic concept *par excellence*—as the strongest identification with Canada on the part of young anglophones.

One national project in Canadian Studies during the 1970's produced materials developed in a unique partnership of academic researchers, geography educators and classroom teachers.[21] These publications were not aimed solely at geography teachers for use in geography courses. They were also intended for use in history and social studies courses.

Canadian geography teachers had sometimes seemed isolationist and defensive—an understandable posture given the long struggle to establish a place for their subject in the curriculum. That many were now more willing to adopt an interdisciplinary perspective bespoke a new found confidence as well as a recognition that teachers of all subjects, including geography, could not ignore the social significance of their disciplines. This trend was reinforced by a renewed concern among university geographers for synthesis, reflecting possibly some reaction against the more analytic systematic emphasis of the 1960's. Never before in Canadian history had there been a greater need to help young people gain an integrated understanding of their vast and complex nation. Geography teachers could justly argue that no other subject area had more to contribute to that understanding and to global understanding.

---

[21] See John WOLFORTH and George S. TOMKINS, "The New Canadian Geography Project", *History and Social Science Teacher*, 12(4) (Summer, 1977), pp. 225-232.

CURRICULUM, GEOGRAPHY, AND THE CANADIAN CONTEXT

F. GEOFFREY JONES
Memorial University of Newfoundland

Curriculum development in Canada has tended to follow North American practices. These practices have attempted to delineate the use of disciplines as clear-cut, precise areas of learning and teaching with reasonably clear boundaries of knowledge. If a single educational term can be identified to describe this situation, "integration" may be that term. Curriculum developers, with the assistance of learning theorists, have endeavoured to perform their tasks such that clear and logical relationships can be seen to exist not only within content areas but also between content areas. Consequently, we have in Canada attempts to link language arts programs with math and science programs, or science programs with math and social studies programs. Further, we have attempts to produce science programs that mix physics, chemistry, and biology content and scientific methodology.

To assist in the organization of such development, documents have been produced that outline, not only scope and sequence of content, but also rationale, objectives (mainly instructional objectives), methods and strategies, sources of resources, and assessment. Such documents have replaced the course outlines or syllabi that prescribed content and gave little if any direction to the teacher as to how the material might or could be used with students. How useful the teacher's guide or outline of syllabus is, remains to be seen. What may be important is the recognition by curriculum developers that something beyond the bland outline of content and prescribed text material was needed. What prompted this "new" turn in curriculum thinking? What were the "needs" that these changes in thinking were attempting to fill? How did the "newer" guides purport to fill these needs? What effects did this newer thinking have upon the presentation of geography as a school subject? These are but a few of a host of questions upon which we could dwell.

I.—CURRICULUM AND GEOGRAPHY

Curriculum thinking in Canada has been influenced by a variety of curriculum theorists. Johnson (1967, p. 130) has indicated,

In view of the shortcomings of the currently popular definition, it is here stipulated that curriculum is a structured series of intended learning outcomes. Curriculum prescribes (or at least anticipates) the results of instruction,

while Neagley and Evans (1967, p. 2) refer to curriculum as,

all the planned experience provided by the school to assist pupils in attaining the designated learning outcomes to the best of their abilities.

Both of these definitions, and others that are related, imply the use of a means-ends model an idea which has permeated the thinking of major curriculum theorists for some time. The model begins by stating performance criteria which will be attained by the student by the conclusion of a lesson or course, and outlines approaches designed to fulfill these performance objectives. The curriculum as such, then becomes a means to an end which is expressed in terms of student attainment, and may well be constrained by the statement of behavioural objectives (as intended learning outcomes) and thus overlook other significant learning that may take place through the curriculum.

For geography, the use of a means-ends model could lead to a limited depth of study by students. Teachers may only provide geographic content and learning experiences that would allow fulfillment of the intended learning outcomes. Self-initiated research into geographic topics could be discouraged because they may not fall into the learning plan. Incidential or related experiences, perhaps arising from a field trip or research in the library, would not be encouraged, and the results of such endeavours, if allowed, may not be acknowledged in the final assessment of student performance.

In another vein, Janzen (1970), a Canadian curriculum specialist, has defined curriculum as,

... the sum total of the school's efforts to influence learning whether in the classroom, on the playground, or out of school. It is everything the students and teachers do under the guidance of the school (pp. 16-17).

Janzen's definition adopts the broad view of curriculum where the behaviours that are produced by the learner are from planned school experiences. While, this definition recognizes input that school and teacher preparation can make to the students learning environment, it does overlook learning experiences that grow out of planned experiences and yet which are related. Tyler (1949) recognized these two major contributions in his work but failed to explicate them clearly in his four fundamental questions as laid out in his book *Basic Principles of Curriculum and Instruction*. These four questions can be arranged in linear fashion to form the following curriculum model.

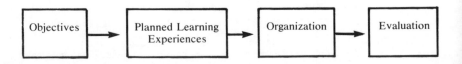

Tyler's ideas are important because they acknowledge that educational personnel can be responsible for making important educational decisions such as:

1) What are the objectives?
2) What are the learning experiences?
3) How can these experiences be effectively and efficiently organized?
and 4) What kinds of evaluation shall be employed?

Such curriculum decision-making processes are congruent with the development of geography as a school experience in that teachers are involved in such processes in Canada (Jones, 1978). Teachers develop lists of objectives, organize and implement learning experiences for their students, and administer evaluations at varying intervals. However, one problem of the Tyler approach, also evident in the practice of the means-ends model, is that evaluation occurs only at the end of instruction and is rarely used for assessing formative instructional performance. Consequently, it becomes difficult to determine whether teacher objectives have been achieved or whether alternative instructional procedures may have been more efficient. Subsequent research into curriculum theories has in the main accommodated this deficiency, particularly in the works of Taba (1962).

Taba (1962) discussed curriculum, as a plan for student learning (p. 11). Such a plan evolved from identification, analysis, and implementation of certain criteria that were related through their contiguity and continuity. She identified seven steps that she saw as producing a more dynamically conceived and planned curriculum. These steps are:

1) Diagnosis of needs.
2) Formulation of objectives.
3) Selection of content
4) Organization of content.
5) Selection of learning experiences.
6) Organization of learning experiences.
7) Determination of what to evaluate and of the ways and means of doing it (p. 12).

Taba's seven steps have been applied within the more general framework of social studies in North America, however, they do lend themselves to aiding development in geography instruction (see Figure 1).

Curricula are designed for student acquisition of knowledge. As students bring a variety of backgrounds to a learning situation it is necessary to determine what gaps or deficiencies are present. Diagnosis, then, becomes the vehicle for identifying where to begin geography instruction with a given population. From the diagnosis of the various inputs into the curriculum (geography—society—student interest etc.) a set of clear and comprehensive objectives can be derived as a

Figure 1

APPLICATION OF TABA'S SEVEN
STEPS TO A GEOGRAPHIC EXAMPLE

Diagnosis of Needs
Geography ◄──► Society ◄──► Student Interests ◄──► Assumptions ◄──►
Values of Geography Instruction

Formative
Assessment

Formulation of Objectives
—based upon perceived needs of geography, society, students, etc.
Both cognitive and affective objectives are needed and should use the
Taxonomies for development.

Formative
Assessment

Selection and Organization of Content
Identification and organization of the scope and sequence of geography
content.
Use of concepts and generalizations as a skeletal structure for the geography program, that will help fulfill objectives of the program.

Formative
Assessment

Selection and Organization of Learning Experiences
Levels of student cognitive and mental preparedness. Availability of resources.
Inter-personal relationships. Methods of presenting geography content
will be used taking into account student backgrounds.

Formative
Assessment

What and How to Evaluate
For Students
Pupils cognitive and affective response to questions
Objective tests of geographical learning
Essay tests
Group and individual projects
Simulation

For Instructional Effectiveness
Pupul scores on tests
Pupil behaviour in classes
Objective teacher observations

foundation. The objectives determine what content is important and how the content can be organized. Statements concerning skill development and affective outcomes would also appear.

However, while selection and organization of the content is founded on the statement of objectives, other criteria interplay; significance of the content selection, validity of the selection, hierarchical and sequential arrangement within and between grades, and decisions about the level of conceptual development to be attained by students need to be considered. Furthermore, the task of selecting and organizing learning experiences requires more than knowledge of learning theory. Such considerations as strategies for concept attainment, implementation of strategies to develop attitudes, availability and use of resources, interpersonal relationship between teacher-student and student-student become important if the objectives are to be fulfilled and students are to be exposed to viable and valuable learning experiences through geography instruction. (See Figure 2 for an example of how the spiral of concept approach may be applied to concepts of geography.)

Finally, we need to plan evaluation. How well have students achieved? What values or attitudes have they acquired, changed, or re-enforced? How effective has instruction been? What changes need to be made in scope and sequence, delivery procedures, resources, skill development exercises? Evaluation thus takes on two forms; effects upon students and effectiveness of instruction. Decisions can be reached about both based upon written and observed student behaviours. A third form of evaluation, formative evaluation, provides for an ongoing evaluation to take place as each step develops. Development of the curriculum thus becomes a systematic task which proceeds only after satisfaction has been attained at each prior step. The enterprise culminates when the program is evaluated in the light of student outcomes and teaching effectiveness.

II.—GEOGRAPHY IN THE CANADIAN CONTEXT

Studies in geography involve people, their environments, and the interactions between the two. Students in Canadian schools have generally acquired first-hand experience of only a small percentage of the earth's surface. Although their opportunities for travel and their exposure to the many means of communication may have been greater than those of previous generations, their world is correspondingly more complex and dynamic. In order to broaden their knowledge of the earth, students need to seek clarification of the patterns and processes that result from the interactions of people and their environments. It is important, therefore, that studies in geography have a definite purpose, maintain clear points of view, and promote precise thinking (Department of Education, Ontario, 1977).

With this philosophy in mind, I propose to examine the current scope of the geography curriculum across Canada. Geography curric-

Figure 2

AN EXAMPLE OF THE SPIRAL
DEVELOPMENT OF THREE KEY GEOGRAPHIC CONCEPTS

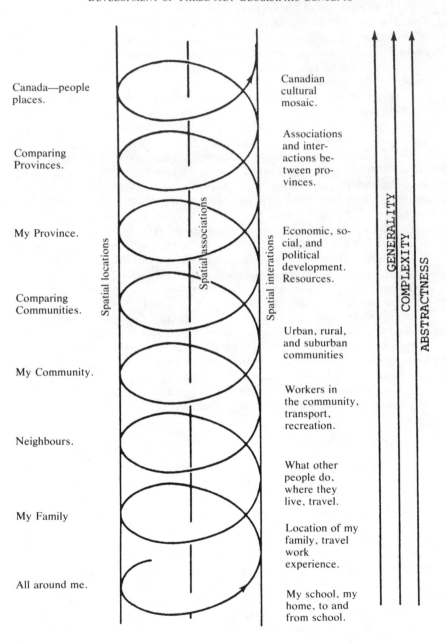

ula in each of the ten provinces are examined individually in order to gain some insight into their diversity. However, some of the information may not reflect the current status of the geography curricula in certain provinces because curriculum guides were either dated or not available in their entirety. The provinces are presented in alphabetical order.

Section I : ALBERTA

According to the *Alberta Social Studies Handbook for 1974*, Alberta's social studies curriculum (Grades I-XII) is premised on the assumption that schools must help students in their quest for a clear, consistent, and defensible system of values. Two inter-related implications of this assumption for social studies instruction stand out: firstly, students must explore and assess the nature of values that influence their personal and social lives; secondly, students must develop the ability to make decisions pertinent to both their individual beings and their roles as active participants in their physical and social environments (Department of Education, Alberta, 1974, p. 5). Geography, holds a dominant place in the rationale of the Alberta social studies curriculum. This is especially true in providing experiences to develop students' understanding of their physical environment and the values that demand attention when that environment is to be used.

The following outline of the Alberta social studies curriculum will help to distinguish the prominent role of geography.

Grade I—*Family Life*

—Analysis of family living through case studies of, such topics as, a contemporary family, a family of long ago, an Afro-Asian family, and other families.

Grade II—*Neighbourhoods*

—Analysis of interactions which occur among, for example, the local neighbourhoods, rural and urban neighbourhoods, neighbourhoods in other cultures.

Grade III—*Comparing People's Communities*

—Comparison and contrast of community life in, for example, a modern-day Indian or Eskimo community and a North American megalopolis; a village in Africa or Asia, and a community in the Pacific, or tropical South America; a Mennonite or Hutterite community and other communities which lend themselves to comparison and contrast.

Grade V—*People in Alberta*

—Historical, economic, sociological and/or geographic analysis of Alberta's people, including comparison and contrast with other world areas that have similar historical, geographic and/or economic bases, for example, Australia, Argentina, U.S.S.R., Middle East oil producers, Western U.S.A. and other areas.

Grade V—*People in Canada*

—Sample studies to analyze historical and/or contemporary life in Canadian regions, for example, people in an Atlantic fishing port, people in a French-Canadian mining town or farm community, people in a St. Lawrence Seaway port, people in an Ontario manufacturing center, people from a Prarie farm or oil town, people in British Columbia forestry industry, and other sample studies.

Grade VI—*Historical Roots of Man*

—Anthropological analysis and social history of early civilizations in, for example, the Mediterranean area, the Far East, the Americas, and Africa.

Grade VII—*Man, Technology and Culture in Pre-Industrial Societies*

—Conceptual understanding of man, technology and culture through case studies of primitive, pre-industrial societies to be selected by teachers and students.

Grade VIII—*Man, Technology and Culture in Afro-Asian Societies*

—Depth studies of societies selected from Africa, Asia (excluding the U.S.S.R.), the Middle East, and the Pacific Islands.

Grade IX—*Man, Technology and Culture in Western Societies*

—Depth studies of societies selected from the Americas (excluding Canada), Europe, all of the U.S.S.R., Australia, and New Zealand.

Grade X—*Canadian Problems*

—Historical, economic, sociological, political and geographic problems facing Canada.

Grade XI—*World Problems and Issues*

—Tradition versus change
—Population and Production

From this description it would seem that geography has a central role in the social studies curriculum of all grade levels. For instance, in Grade Two the focus is on various types of neighbourhoods. The student is introduced to the concepts of urban and rural, which are important concepts in geography. By Grade Nine the student is studying more complex geographical concepts applied to various regions of the world.

An analysis of the role of geography in the Alberta social studies curriculum indicates that it is an evolving discipline. The student is first introduced to his own neighbourhood, then his community, neighbouring communities, and as he advances from grade level to grade level, he is introduced to geographical knowledge on a regional, provincial, national, and international basis. Further, conceptual development occurs using a concrete to abstract pattern in keeping with the student's cognitive progress.

Section II: BRITISH COLUMBIA

According to the *Elementary Social Studies Curriculum Guide 1974* for British Columbia, the social studies program is designed to encourage children to organize their inquiry, provide them with the means of understanding the world around them and help them to examine and consider values, thus beginning the process of developing their own values system (Department of Education, British Columbia; 1971, p. 2).

The following overview of the British Columbia Social Studies programme highlights the role played by Geography.

Year I, II and III—*The Student and his Environment*

The first three years of the social studies program are interrelated. In the first year the child is introduced to the concept of the family. He learns about size, composition, social and economic position, and ethnic and cultural backgrounds of families. In the second year the child's knowledge is expanded to include the role of the family in the community. The child begins to realize that people must depend upon the services of each other for such things as food, fuel and transportation. By year three the child's environment is expanded to include interaction between different communities. The emphasis is on the relationships which exist *between* communities and between communities and their environments.

Year IV

People as cultural beings is the focus of year four. The overall topic for study is the early cultures of North America with emphasis upon how the environment, including climate, affects their lives.

Year V—*A Study of Canada*

In year five students are introduced to a regional study of Canada. Selected communities across Canada are studied, e.g. a fishing community, a farming community, a mining community, a lumbering community, and others. Students should become aware of how Canadians live and how the environment affects the way they live.

Year VI and VII

The global view of man in major cultural groupings is presented in year six by studying culture realms, which is expanded to include culture stages in year seven. The social studies program does not provide a further description of the program offered in these two years.

However, from the brief description offered there seems to be a major emphasis on cultural geography.

Information was not available on the secondary social studies program in British Columbia. However, the brief description of the curriculum offered at the elementary level helps to provide some insight into the status of Geography in the curriculum at least at this level. Students in elementary social studies are introduced to a variety of geographic concepts such as: kinds of communities, relationship between communities and their environment, transportation, communication, and climate. Also, students are introduced to such geographic skills as map reading and map making.

Section III—MANITOBA

The underlying philosophy of the Manitoba social studies curriculum is that social studies, should lead students not only to a knowledge of how men and women live in various parts of the world, but also to an understanding of why they live the way they do (Department of Education, Manitoba, 1973, p. 5).

Geography provides students with the knowledge of people from various parts of the world, and also with an understanding of how people live the way they do. The significance of geography within this curriculum is readily understood by the following outline.

Grade I—*The Home, The School, The Immediate Community*

The course centers on a study of the child's home, his school, and his immediate community. It attempts to compare the lives of city and country children. Each child studies his own area first and then compares this with the alternative type of community.

Grade II—*People of my Community*

This program expands to the larger community and is centered about the people living in it and the occupations they pursue. The program is to help students understand and appreciate the interdependence of people in a community.

Grade III—*Prehistoric Man, Plains Indians, Canadian Eskimos*

The general aim of the course is to show the student how man was able to adapt himself to, and to modify, his environment. The geographic aspects of this course involve understanding the physical environment and how man adapted to it.

Grade IV—*Communities Around the World*

The following group of communities is studied: River Communities, Mountain Communities, Island (or Peninsula) Communities, countries of origin of people in the local community. Some geographic concepts that are studied include rivers, source, mouth, tributary, delta, plains, hills, mountains, peaks, valleys, glaciers, plateau, island, peninsula, coastline, bay, gulf, ocean, and sea.

Grade V—*Sample Studies*

Students use sample studies of the following: An Urban Community—Winnipeg, A Mixed Farming Area, a Northern Community, A Manufacturing Town, a Coastal Fishing Community, a Community of a Mountainous Area. Students also conduct a geographic study of Manitoba, a geographic study of North America, and a study of the Political and Physical Geography of Canada.

Grade VI—*Canadian History*

As an outgrowth of the grade five geography course, the grade six program traces the historical development of Canada, with consistent reference being made to the concepts and understandings established in previous grades.

From Grade VII onwards geography and history are taught as two separate disciplines.

Grade VII—*Geography of Europe*

The aims of Geography are to enable students to visualize accurately the areas they are studying, to develop a willingness to try and understand the ways of peoples in other lands, and to introduce the concept of world citizenship. Also, students will develop skills to read from various types of maps and to relate map information to areas being studied.

Grade VIII—*Indian Sub-continent, U.S.S.R., China, Japan*

In this course students are given an indepth analysis of selected geographical features of the above countries. The course introduces the student to a number of advanced concepts in geography. Some of these are high and low pressure cells, continental and oceanic winds, relation between population distribution and relief, and others.

Grade IX—*Geography of the Southern Continents*

In this course students study various regions in the southern continents. Two approaches are used. First, a regional study which delineates a political region (Brazil), is used, and second, a geographical region (the Congo Basin) is identified. The second approach looks at the climatic-vegetation zones in each continent, e.g. the tropical forest areas in South America, Africa, and Australia and then focus in on the Congo Basin as a regional study.

There was no information available on the Manitoba Geography curriculum beyond Grade IX. However, the description of the program in the preceeding grades helps to provide an understanding of the significant role played by geography in the Manitoba social studies curriculum. Like many provinces, the Manitoba social studies curriculum is designed to give the student knowledge of the expanding physical and human environment.

Section IV : NEW BRUNSWICK

The underlying philosophy of the New Brunswick social studies curriculum is that man can, through reason, solve the problems of his neighbourhood, country, and the world. The paramount role of geography in this underlying philosophy is evident. If man is to help solve the problems of his neighbourhood, country, and the world, he must first have a geographic understanding of each of these (Department of Education, New Brunswick, 1976, 0.25).

The intended idea of the curriculum is to emphasize, wherever possible, the community concept—the inter-relations of communities in our own country, and the inter-relations of countries in the world.

With this in mind, the following description attempts to delineate the role of geography in the New Brunswick social studies curriculum.

Grade I—*Home and School*

A study of the daily life of the student's local community, i.e., his family and school.

Grade II—*The Community*

A study of the home community of the child and a comparison of it with communities with which he may be familiar, the work carried on by the various people of the community and the value of work to everyone in the community.

Grade III—*Children in Other Lands*

A study, from the standpoint of the child, of life in far-away places; learning how climate and other geographical conditions affect community life and so produce trade between different communities.

Grade IV—*Communities of Yesterday and Today*

A study of selected early communities and a comparison with present-day living conditions in New Brunswick to show how man has gradually improved his conditions through the ages.

Grades V and VI—*Canada and Her Neighbours*

A study of the geography and development of Canada and the United States.

Grade VII

Geography in grade seven pays special attention to map study, the living habits and customs of different ethnic groups, and the effects of physical conditions upon the way of life of people.

Grade VIII

The geography part of the course covers Africa, Asia, and Australia. Emphasis is placed upon the relationship of land, climate, and man.

Grade IX—*Twin Heritages*

The course deals with the British and French heritage of Canada. Besides the historical and political emphasis, there is a stress on the importance of the geographical setting of the two cultures in Canada.

There is a separation of the geography and history courses in the New Brunswick high school social studies curriculum.

Grade X—*Geography 102*

This course offers an introduction to physical and human geography. There are four basic units: The Topographical Map, the Landscape, Weather and Climate, and Human Geography.

Grade XI—*Geography 112*

This course offers a study of selected regional areas. Some of the regions studied are: the Great Plains, a geographical study of a rich agricultural area, a region of phenomenal geographic change, e.g. the Moscow Region, an industrial Region, and a River Valley Region.

Grade XII—*Geography 122*

This course offers a study of the geography of Canada indicating the interaction of three basic systems or environments—the societal, the physical, and the artificial. The course is designed to give the student an understanding of the processes of social and economic changes occurring in Canada and of their relevance for the student as a Canadian citizen. The basic units of the course are: the Canadian Setting, the Regional Studies, and Research Themes.

The New Brunswick geography curriculum adopts an evolutionary approach. In the early years stress is put on the local environment of the student and is then expanded to a world view in later years. During the first nine years geography is part of the general social studies curriculum, however, during the last three years of high school geography is a separate subject.

Section V: NEWFOUNDLAND

According to *A Teaching Guide for Social Studies Grades K-6 for 1973-74* the social studies program purports to hold a key position in the primary grades in Newfoundland. It draws upon the content of geography, history, economics, sociology, anthropology, citizenship. Conservation and current events. The purpose of the program is to provide the student with the knowledge, understanding, appreciation, and values the student needs in order to eventually take his or her place as a worthwhile citizen in society (Department of Education, Newfoundland; 1973, p. 1). The student is supposed to be introduced to selected geographical concepts by studying his or her immediate environment of the home, school, and community.

Grade IV—*World Communities*

The student extends his or her interests beyond the limits of the neighbourhood and local community through a detailed study of various world regions. Some of the regions studied are : Tundra, Tropical Rainforest, Deserts, and High Plateaus.

By the end of the fourth grade there is a separation of history and geography in the Newfoundland social studies curriculum. This is unlike other provinces, where the separation does not happen until the secondary level.

Grade V—*Geography of Newfoundland and Labrador*

The course is designed to develop an understanding of how geographic factors influence living in various areas of Newfoundland and how the people of various areas achieve their needs. Skills in using maps and globes effectively in dealing with problems of area, location, distance, elevation, density population, travel routes, products, rainfall, vegetation, and the relationship between surface features and living conditions are also emphasized.

Grade VI—*Canada : This Land of Ours*

The course is designed to help the student to understand and appreciate people who live in other regions of Canada and to become more conscious of the fact that all Canadians have the same basic needs. However, they may be met in different ways which are determined by location, physical features, climate and the culture of the people who live across Canada.

Grade VII—*Introducing Earth*

The object of the course is to identify the main regions and peoples of the world, stressing the way people live, the problems presented by certain types of environments, the earlier methods of coping with them, and the further problems created by the impact of western civilization and technology upon the way of life of other people.

Grade VIII—*Introducing Earth Part II*

This is a continuation of the grade seven geography course. Students have the opportunity to pursue regional studies of the following areas : the U.S.A.—The Warm South, South of Capricorn, Monsoon Lands of Asia, and Deserts and Savannahs of the World.

Grade IX—*Canada : A New Geography*

This course affords the student the opportunity to pursue a geographical study of Canada, by identifying a variety of concepts and interrelationships which aids the student in seeing how each region of Canada is dependent upon the rest of Canada. The course discusses some of the problems facing the country, e.g. Conservation, farming problems, Regional Planning and Development, Rural poverty, Urban planning, and Water resources.

Grade X—*Elements of Geography*

This is basically a physical geography course. The course is divided into two sections: the first deals with the earth as a planet, and the second deals with the form of the earth.

Grade XI—*Elements of Geography*

This is a continuation of the grade ten course. However, there is an emphasis put on human geography as well as physical geography. The topics to be studied are: climate, climatic regions and their effects upon man, economic geography, and population.

While geography receives considerable attention in the Newfoundland Social Studies program it is treated as a separate subject. In other provinces such a separation does not happen before the secondary level.

The primary social studies program is designed to give the student a knowledge of his immediate environment. However, by grade four the child is introduced to world geography which seems to be a significant jump considering the limited knowledge gained at the primary level. This means that there may be some degree of disunity in the Newfoundland geography curriculum.

Section VI: Nova Scotia

The elementary social studies program in Nova Scotia is not only geographically and historically oriented, but also includes aspects of sociology, anthropology, economics and political science. The program centers on six main themes, sequenced to begin with areas of study familiar to the child—self, family, community, region. It then reaches out to look at other families, communities, regions, both in and outside Canada, leading to an in-depth analysis of the Atlantic Provinces and its people.

The themes in sequence are:

Year I—Orientation; Year II—Families; Year III—Communities; Year IV—Communities and Regions; Year V—Man in his Changing Environment; Year VI—Canada and the World's Peoples; Year VII—The Atlantic Provinces (Department of Education, Nova Scotia; 1977).

By grade seven there is a formal separation of history and geography.

Grade VII—*Geography of Canada*

This course gives the students an overall view of Canada, a more detailed study of regions, and an opportunity to do in-depth studies of selected areas and industries within the country. Studies will include geographical and climatic factors, and various ways people live and earn their living.

Grade VIII—*Geography of the United States*

The course gives students an understanding of the geography of the United States and of those factors which most affect Canadians. Wherever possible the geographical links between Canada and the United States are developed. Extensive use is suggested for visual and graphic materials—air and ground photos, large and small maps, and pictures.

Grade IX—*Geography of Europe*

This course allows students to gain an overall view of Europe, and then to undertake in-depth studies of smaller areas representative of large areas. Also, studies should include geographical and climatic factors and the ways people live and earn their living. Extensive use is made of maps and photos.

Grade X—*Geography of Asia*

This course provides students with an understanding of the geographical and climatic factors of Asia, and a knowledge of the way people live and earn their living.

Grade XI—*Physical Geography*

Extensive laboratory work in the form of map usage, plotting, graphing, aerial photo studies is an essential part of this course. Field trips are considered very important for giving students first hand knowledge of key geographical features as they relate to the landscape.

Grade XII—*Geography of Canada*

This course provides students with a more sophisticated understanding of the effect of geographical and climatic factors in the various regions of Canada. Extensive use is made of geography resource books, geographical terminology, photo interpretation, cartographic methods, and geography simulations.

Like the social studies curriculum for many of the provinces, the Nova Scotia social studies curriculum in the early years is concerned with the child's immediate environment. The child is first introduced to such geographic concepts as communities, the way people live, and man and his environment. In the elementary school years the studies range from the study of the student's home community in the first years to the study of the Atlantic provinces in the late elementary school years. At the secondary level geography is studied as a separate discipline. The student's environment is expanded to include the geography of other countries, as well as in-depth studies into selected aspects of Canadian Geography. Also, there is considerable emphasis placed upon the use of the various tools used by the geographer.

Section VII: ONTARIO

At the primary level (ages 6 to 11) geography is taught in a broad field approach called social studies and natural science, and not as a separate discipline. In this way the child is introduced to the basic concepts of geography in describing and explaining the society in which he lives and the natural world which surrounds him. Studies at this stage concentrate first on the familiar local area, move out to include more distant communities and finally to selected areas around the world.

Geography is first introduced as a distinct discipline in Ontario schools at the intermediate level (ages 12 to 15). Specifically geographical studies at this level concentrate on the concept of the earth as the home of man, analysing the interaction of physical and human influences on the landscape.

The study of geography as a discipline is taken further at the secondary level (ages 16 to 18). At this stage systematic subdivisions of geography are introduced: the physical geography of land, sea and air and the human geography of societies, and economic and urban areas. These are then recombined in the study of regions, ending with an examination of Canada as a separate geographic entity and then as part of the world (Dilley and Heggie, 1975, p. 29).

The stages of geographical education in Ontario thus follow a consciously-designed pattern; beginning with local awareness, expanding to consider the world and returning to more detailed local studies.[1]

The Ontario social studies curriculum and the role of geography in that curriculum indicates that the program is designed to give the student and evolving social studies education. Like Alberta and a number of other provinces, Ontario's geography curriculum starts with the student's immediate surroundings (home, school, community) and expands to provide a broader view (province, regions, country, international).

Section VIII: PRINCE EDWARD ISLAND

In the Prince Edward Island curriculum guide for social studies it is stated that social studies is a term given to the area of school curriculum which assists the child to develop an understanding of human relationships. The subjects from which its content is drawn includes history and geography, and elements of sociology, anthro-

---

[1] See R. S. DILLEY, and B. C. HEGGIE, "Ontario System of Education", Monograph, Ontario Association for Geographic and Environmental Education, Issue No. 3, 1975, for a more complete overview of the Ontario geography program.

pology, political science, and economics. Stress is placed on the inter-relationships of the various branches of study. It is clear that geography, like history, is central to the curriculum.

The program in the primary grades centers attention on the individual in his immediate surroundings, and by the secondary school years the student is presented with a picture of his worldwide surrounding (Department of Education, Prince Edward Island, 1977, p. 26).

The description which follows should help to give the reader a greater understanding of the role of geography in the curriculum.

Grade I—*Our Homes and Families, Our School, Our Neighbourhood, The Farm, Special Days.*

The student is introduced to such concepts as the home, family neighbourhood, and farm. With the use of activities such as field trips, discussions, constructions and pre-map work, the student is introduced to these concepts.

Grade II

This program is a continuation and expansion of interests, content, and procedures outlined in grade one. The child's scope of experience is now broadened to include friends and neighbours in a widening community.

Grade III

The Grade III program further extends those interests, concepts, attitudes, and skills begun in previous grades. Relation to the community is broadened to the province, its places of interest; its geographical aspects and its historical background.

Grade IV

Grade four is considered a transition stage in pupil growth. Students are required to study a unit on Canada—looking at historical, geographic, political and cultural aspects of the country. Also, students are introduced to people in other parts of the world.

Grade V

Two main sections are identified : (1) a brief survey of Canada as a whole, noting general physical features, divisions into provinces, and population distribution; (2) a more detailed study of the Atlantic Provinces and Quebec; background of discovery and settlement, physical features, large centers, resources, and industries.

Grade VI

Grade VI is a continuation of the program of the previous years. There is more emphasis put on map and globe concepts and skills. The first part of the course deals with Canada and her neighbours and the second deals with the historical, geographic, and socio-economic features of Prince Edward Island.

Grade VII

By grade seven there is a clear division between history and geography. Both are offered as separate courses. In the geography course students are given some understanding of the different regions and peoples of Canada.

Grade VIII

The grade eight geography course introduces the students to the geography of The British Isles and Germany.

Grade IX

In grade nine students study world geography. They study such countries as the United States and Latin America and are also introduced to concepts concerning climate and the physical landscape.

Grade X

Grade ten geography students study regional geography. The students study regions such as deserts, coniferous forest regions, grasslands, and monsoon lands.

Grade XI

The grade eleven geography course gives students an in-depth study of Canadian geography.

Grade XII

In grade twelve students study world geography in such areas as Europe, U.S.S.R., Asia, Africa, North America, and South America.

The above outline indicates that geography is central to the Prince Edward Island social studies curriculum. In many ways the geography curriculum is similar to that of other provinces in that there is a tendency in the early years to give the student an understanding of his immediate environment such as the school, neighbourhood, and community. However, by the middle school and secondary grades, students are introduced to provincial, regional, national, and world geography.

Section IX : QUEBEC

The Quebec elementary school social studies curriculum does not make a distinction between history and geography as separate disciplines and foregoes the practice of including one or the other in the elementary school years. In the elementary school curriculum, these disciplines are considered as elements of a more comprehensive area of study, i.e. the social sciences applied to observations of what is generally referred to as the environment (Department of Education Quebec, 1974, p. 31).

Again, like many other provinces, there is a separation of geography and history at the high school level.

The following description of the areas of study will help to explain the role of geography in schools in Quebec.

Grade I—*The Home and Family, The School, Orientations between Home and School*

These topics deal with the notion of the acquisition of space; the home and the school serve as points of reference for learning about orientation and distance.

Grade II—*Basic Needs and Services*

Students deal with the basic needs of and services to the inhabitants of the local Environment. For example, they deal with the origin and sources of certain foodstuffs.

Grade III—*Land Transportation Systems and Physical Habitat*

Students deal with various modes of transportation such as roads (gravel and pavement), railroads, and subways. Also, there is emphasis on the types of vehicles used with each of these modes of transportation. Further, students learn about the relationship between physical habitats and architectural patterns such as the different types of buildings found in different places. Plans and maps are used to introduce students to the notion of regional environment defined as a geographic space which is larger in area than the local environment.

Grade IV—*The Inhabited Areas of Quebec*

The geographic horizons of students at this grade level is broadened so as to sensitize them to the distances which separate the various localities of the province, their names and their sizes. Comparisons are made with the pupils' own locality. Also the notion of geographic space is consolidated by exploring the production, transportation, and consumption of foodstuffs.

Grade V—*Navigation, Railways, Industry in Canada, Ways of Life in New France, the Fall of New France*

Students at this grade level have their horizons expanded to Canada as a whole. Quebec becomes the reference point for comparisons with the rest of the country. Finally, a series of topics dealing with industry in various parts of Canada are studied.

Grade VI—*The Airways, Areas of the Americas, The Earth and the Moon, The Fur Trade, The Lumber Trade*

At this grade level, the study of the ways in which airways replace roads, railways and seaways to illustrate the breakdown of transportation barriers between areas of the world and finally, the earth itself, will become the point of reference for an initiation into inter-planetary space studies. The two themes dealing with Canadian history require students to consider aspects of geography, economics, ethnography, and sociology.

As with other provinces, there is a separation of history and geography at this point in the curriculum at least for the English-language schools.

Grade VII—*Introduction to Geography*

This course has two essential aspects; one scientific, and the other technical and practical. The scientific aspect involves a study of the various interrelated elements of the "landscape" (both physical and human) beginning with the local environment before proceeding to the investigation of other regions. Both technical and practical aspect introduce students to, among other things, some of the instruments used by geographers such as the thermograph, barograph, weather-vane, compass and steroscope; graphical representation of information (plans, diagrams, sketches); the use of topographic maps; the observation and explanation of photographs.

Grade VIII—*Regional Geography of the World*

The objectives of the course are to initiate students to an understanding of the world map, and to enable students to learn about the characteristic features of certain countries. The following geographical areas are studied; Europe, Asia, Africa, South and Central America, North America.

Grade IX—*Geography of Canada*

The aim of this course is to provide the basic elements which will enable students to explain the activities of Canadians. The students must be able to explain the relationships between a natural region and the types of economic activity found in that region. The course is organized in the following manner (1) natural environment—structure, landforms, natural regions, climates, natural vegetation, soils; (2) human activities—population, primary, secondary and tertiary activities, exploitation of sources and energy; (3) Quebec—agriculture, industry and distribution of cities, the Montreal region, current economic problems.

Grade X—*The Great Powers and International Exchanges*

An objective of the course is to make students aware of how countries depend on each other, through a study of the phenomenon of produce distribution resulting in a system of exchanges between countries. The course deals with the following areas : countries with a capitalist economy; countries with a collectivist economy; food resources of the world; power resources of the world.

Grade XI—*Physical and Human Geography*

The aims of the course include having students learn the various elements of physical and human geography, expanding their knowledge of physical and human geography, and developing their mastery of the skills and methods of geography; to have the students recognize and extend their understanding of the narrow links existing between these various elements; to develop the students understanding of the interrelatedness of geographic phenomena.

The above description indicates that geography plays a significant part in the overall social studies curriculum of Quebec. Again, as in many other provinces, students first learn about their own communities, and this is expanded to a world view by the later grades. Students are also required to do an in-depth study into various regions in Canada and elsewhere. However, study about the Province of Quebec forms the foundation for the study of other geographic areas.

Section X—SASKATCHEWAN

Social studies deals with special questions about man's way of living; how he lives; where he lives; what has happened to him; how he deals with society; how he makes decisions for group living; how groups affect one another; how the individual and his group interact. (Department of Education, Saskatchewan, 1968, p. 2). It seems that the study of geography should be central to such a social studies program. Geography is certainly significant in dealing with man's way of living. Further the Saskatchewan social studies program is based upon the assumption that social studies is a global study of man in time and place.

Since the only available information on the Saskatchewan social studies program is for the late 1960's, it is possible that many of the programs have changed since then. However, an overview of the curriculum offered at that time may help to shed some light on the Saskatchewan geography curriculum.

Grade I—*Adaptation of students to their Environment*

The basic objective of the course is to help students realize that they depend on other people in the home, school and neighbourhood. Some of the geographic skills that should develop at this stage are: cardinal directions and maps as models of the earth's surface.

Grade II

The grade two social studies program is basically a continuation of the Grade 1 program. Besides studying the home, school, and neighbourhood, students are introduced to the farm, town, city, and homes of other people. These are important geographic concepts for students. They are introduced to the characteristics that help to distinguish a farm, a town, or city. Also, by studying the homes of other people, the student can see how people in other countries live.

Grade III—*Adaptation of People to Environmental Forces of Nature*

Again, this is a continuation of the work completed in the previous two years. The objectives of the course are expanded to include realization that climate, soil and location influence the lives of people, understanding the effects of environment upon the habits of people, acquisition of an interest in people in other parts of the world, understanding the ways in which the people of Saskatchewan make a living, understanding the contributions and relationships of people in different parts of the world.

Information on the Saskatchewan social studies curriculum was not available for grades IV, V and VI. However, it may be assumed that there was a continuation of the curriculum offered at the earier elementary grade levels.

Grade VII—*A Geographic Study of Regions of the Eastern Hemisphere*

In this course, the regional approach was used. Specific regions were selected for study because they were typical of selected environments. Concepts of the physical environment that influenced man—land relations such as climate, topography, soils, and vegetation were introduced.

Grade VIII—*Canada's Heritage*

This is basically a history course dealing with Canada's heritage and growth to nationhood. Besides studying historical events, students investigate environmental, cultural and political factors within Canada. Concepts in human geography play a significant part.

Grade IX—*The Origins of Western Civilization and Culture*

This is basically a history course. Geography in grades X, XI, and XII in Saskatchewan is offered as a separate discipline in the social studies curriculum.

Grade X—*Physical Geography*

In this course, students are introduced to an extensive study of physical geography. They deal with concepts such as landscape, climate, topography, landform, and a variety of other concepts related to physical geography. Also, students learn about some of the tools used by the physical geographer in his work.

Grade XI—*Regional Differences in North America*

In this course, students are provided with an understanding of the broad regional differences, both cultural and physical, which occur within the North American continent with an attempt in the last unit to show the place of North America in the world setting.

Grade XII—*Geography of Population*

This course follows from the studies outlined in the grade ten and eleven courses. The intent of the course is to acquaint and explain to students the basic distributions of physical and cultural phenomena over the earth's surface. Some of the units of the course include: the geography of population, the western industralized world, tropical settlement, the pioneer fringe, northern settlement, and political geography.

From the above description, the role of geography in the Saskatchewan social studies curriculum is clear. At first, the student is introduced to his immediate environment, and in later grades this is expanded to the broader environment of the province, country, region, and the world. Also, in the later grades the student pursues in-depth studies into physical, cultural, human, and political geography.

SUMMARY AND CONCLUSIONS

The theory and practice of curriculum development in the social studies in North America has been strongly influenced by the work of Hilda Taba. Application of her seven steps has led to searches for needs, statements of objectives, outlines of content, selections of learning experiences, and evaluation procedures. Most of these procedures can be handled by teachers despite the strictures of time and availability of materials.

Geography curriculum, as a major contributing partner to the social studies program in the various provinces of Canada, has been able to adapt Taba's principles most effectively. The conceptual nature of the discipline provides a sound learning base for students. Place, areal differentiation, man, and other such concepts allow students to understand the relationships that exist between man and his environment. Such interwoven conceptual development using geography is plainly evident in the social studies program across Canada.

Based upon the objectives outlined in the various curriculum guides in the provinces, an overview of the geography curricula has been presented to provide some insight into the scope of geography content in Canadian schools. From this overview, a number of important points were revealed: (1) during the elementary school years, geography is an integrated part of the social studies program in most provinces, but at the secondary level there is a separation of the disciplines; (2) most provinces seem to have an evolving geography curriculum; i.e. students are first presented with a study of their immediate environment, which is expanded into a world environmental view in later grades; (3) there seems to be significant stress placed upon both physical and human geography, with particular emphasis on the interrelationships between people and their environments.

Finally, there are similarities and differences in geography curricula across Canada. For instance, in Alberta geography is an integrated part of the social studies program from I-XII, whereas in Newfoundland, there is a separation as early as the fourth grade. However, as already mentioned, geography in all the provinces seems to place an important emphasis upon the relationship between man and his environment. While the design of geography curricula across Canada may be acceptable to teachers of geography and educators in most cases, if these curricula are to help students acquire the goals intended by the curriculum developers, then the methods of teaching and instructional materials must also be considered as of paramount importance if we are to have geographically informed citizens in the future. To this extent Canada may be seen as a leader in geographic education.

REFERENCES

Alberta Social Studies Handbook 1974, Province of Alberta, Department of Education, 1974.

Curriculum Guidelines for Geography, Department of Education, Ontario, 1977.

DILLEY, R. S., and REGGIE, B. C., "Ontario System of Education", *Monograph*, Ontario Association for Geographic and Environmental Education, Issue No. 3, 1975.

Elementary School Curriculum Guide for Divisions II and III, Department of Education, Saskatchewan, 1965.

Elementary Social Studies (Years 1, 2, 3), Department of Education, British Columbia, 1971.

Experience in Decision-Making : Elementary Social Studies Handbook, Department of Education, Alberta, 1974.

Handbook for English-Language Schools of Quebec, Department of Education, Quebec, 1974.

The History and Social Science Teacher, Vol 13, No. 3, Spring, 1978.

JANZEN, H., *Curriculum Change in a Canadian Context*, Quance Lectures (Toronto: Gage Educational Publishing, 1970).

JOHNSON, M., "A Model for curriculum and instruction", *Educational Theory*, 17 (April, 1967), pp. 127-140.

JONES, F. Geoffrey, *Geography Teaching in Canadian Schools* (St. John's Memorial University of Newfoundland, 1978).

Junior High School Social Studies Curriculum Guide, Department of Education, Alberta, 1970.

Manitoba Social Studies Curriculum Guide 1974, Department of Education, Manitoba 1974.

NEAGLEY, R. L., and EVANS, N. D., *Handbook for Effective Supervision of Instruction* (Englewood Cliffs, NJ : Prentice Hall, 1976).

Program of Studies, Department of Education, Manitoba, 1973.

Program of Studies in the Schools of Nova Scotia, Department of Education, Nova Scotia, 1977.

Program of Studies, Department of Education, Newfoundland, 1977.

Program of Studies for the Elementary Schools, Department of Education, Prince Edward Island, 1973.

Social Studies Syllabus, Department of Education, New Brunswick, 1976.

Social Studies Grades 7-8, 1973-74, Department of Education, Newfoundland, 1973.

Social Studies Curriculum Guide, Department of Education, Prince Edward Island, 1977.

Social Studies Handbook, Department of Education, Saskatchewan, 1968.

TABA, H., *Curriculum Development: Theory and Practice* (New York: Harcourt, Brace, and World, 1962).

TABA, H. Durkin, M.C., FRAENKEL, J.R., and McNAUGHTON, A.H., *A Teacher's Handbook to Elementary Social Studies* (Reading, Mass.,; Addison-Wesley Publishing Co., 1971).

Teaching Guide for Social Studies Grades K-6 for 1973-74, Department of Education, Newfoundland, 1973.

TYLER, R. W., *Basic Principles of Curriculum and Instruction* (Chicago: University of Chicago Press, 1950).

TEACHING GEOGRAPHY IN THE ELEMENTARY SCHOOL

IVAN CASSIDY
Acadia University

For a balanced perspective on geography-teaching in Canadian elementary schools today, the topic needs to be viewed against the backcloth of recent developments in the field of social studies education throughout North America.

Following a period of widespread and often mordant criticism of the weaknesses of the educational system attributed to the "progressive movement", and in the wake of the Sputnik furore of the late 1950's, the decade of the sixties saw the emergence of many significant curricular changes in the United States, including what came to be described as "the social studies revolution".

The seminal thinking behind most of the curricular change was that of Jerome Bruner, who in two short, brilliantly written books— *The Process of Education* (1960) and *Toward a Theory of Instruction* (1967) expounded the concept of the "Spiral curriculum". The framework of the school curriculum, he argued, should consist of the key concepts of the scholarly disciplines; young children as well as older ones are capable of understanding the key concepts, provided they are presented in an appropriate way, an accumulation or "spiral" of learning can develop in the pupils' minds as they continue to encounter the concepts in various forms throughout the successive stages of their elementary and secondary schooling. According to Bruner, "The cultivation of a sense of connectedness is the heart of the matter... So much of social studies till now has been a congeries of facts. We should like to make the study more rational, more amenable to the use of the mind at large than mere memorizing."[1]

During the sixties' many school subjects and programmes were critically re-assessed. Social studies came under the scrutiny of the American Council of Learned Societies. The United States Department of Health, Education and Welfare initiated more than fifty research projects related to "Project Social Studies". Social scientists as well as scholars in other disciplines became involved in curriculum development, and there was widespread acceptance of the idea that the content of social studies in the schools should include key

---

[1] Jerome S. BRUNER, *Toward a Theory of Instruction* (Cambridge, Mass : Harvard University Press), 1967, p. 96.

concepts and generalizations of the social sciences in addition to history and geography. If social studies were thus broadened, students would be more capable of understanding man's relation to man and to his environment, and would learn to deal more effectively with the problems of the contemporary world.

As a consequence, throughout the 1970's conceptually-oriented curricula have been developed and implemented at both the elementary and the secondary school levels, with an emphasis on inductive, inquiry-centred teaching methods. An increased concern for the teaching of values and valuing has been apparent. Much emphasis has been placed on the development of skills—on the process of knowing, critical thinking and problem-solving. There has also been concern for more flexible and efficient teaching procedures, leading to the growth of a cornucopia of new instructional materials and learning resources of all kinds.

These trends have characterised the vigorous activity in social studies education which has been going on throughout Canada since the 1960's. In this connection, a publication that received acclaim among social studies educators and had formative influence on curriculum change in Canada was Bruce R. Joyce's *Strategies for Elementary Social Science Education*[2]. The central thesis he propounded was that elementary social studies should be centred on the child's social world, that he should be assisted in studying social topics in such a way that he progressively learns to apply—not merely memorize—the intellectual tools of the social sciences. Joyce saw three goals directing the social studies: (1) humanistic education, enabling the child to understand his own personal experience and find meaning in life; (2) citizenship education, preparing him "To participate effectively in the dynamic life of his society"; (3) intellectual education, assisting him to acquire the analytic ideas and problem-solving tools of the social sciences, so that with increasing maturity he learns "to ask fruitful questions and examine critical data in social situations."

Accordingly he recommended that the curriculum be built around "organizing concepts" drawn from the social sciences. He envisaged a common content giving the child an opportunity to gain different perspectives on the world by way of each discipline, the integrity of each being preserved while avoiding the need for separate courses.

As a reference point for selecting content, Joyce used the concept of the human group. Content should focus on human behaviour, particularly in human relations. Human beings relate to one another largely in groups—history on the history of groups, political science on political relationships between groups, sociology and an-

---

[2]   Bruce R. JOYCE, *Strategies for Elementary Social Science Education* (SRA) 1965. For comment, see George S. TOMKINS, "The Social Studies—An Interdisciplinary Approach Valid for All Levels", in *Monday Morning*, June-July 1968; also the issue of December 1968, p. 40.

thropology on the forms and functions of human groups, economics on group efforts to deal with the problems of production, distribution and consumption of wealth, and geography on human groups in terms of their distribution and varied milieus.

Four basic sources from which content could be selected were : (1) the social life of the students themselves as they interact in and out of school; (2) the society in which the students live (from the level of the local community to the national level); (3) contemporary cultures rather than the students' own; (4) the history of human society. These sources suggest an excellent framework for any modern social studies curriculum.

Joyce advocated organizing each year of his curriculum around no more than three or four "depth studies", chosen from his general sources of content and developed in terms of the organizing concepts drawn from the whole range of social sciences. A useful feature of his book was the attempt to relate the proposed teaching strategies to modern learning theories and to Piaget's research on concept development. Noteworthy also was the successful combining of child-centred, social-centred, and subject-centred viewpoints. It was clear that Joyce's approach was able to invest the traditional social studies curriculum at the elementary school level with much more analytical rigour than it had hitherto possessed.

Comprehensive revision of the elementary as well as the secondary social studies curricula has been carried out in nearly all the provinces of Canada in recent years. A few examples will suffice to indicate the nature of the main changes introduced. In the province of Quebec, the Ministry of Education issued a circular in 1971 entitled "The New Orientation Proposed for the Teaching of the Social Sciences in the Elementary School". It stated,

> This circular makes no distinction between History and Geography as separate disciplines and foregoes the practice of including one or the other in the elementary school curriculum for a given academic year. In the elementary school curriculum these disciplines are to be considered as elements in a more comprehensive area of study : the Social Sciences, applied to the observation of *Reality* from a physical, historical, economic, social or human point of view; in other words, the observation of what is generally referred to as the Environment or "Milieu".[3]

In one of a series of teachers' guides for the province of Quebec, outlining in detail the rationale and methodology of the "new orientation" to social studies, the following explanation is given :

> The old programme divided reality into separate compartments; the new programme attempts to see reality globally through an analysis of as many different points of view as possible. There are many advantages to this approach. First, it allows the teacher to work from the child himself, his environment, his interests, and to gradually lead him to a discovery of the world. Then, rather than stressing rote learning, it puts the accent on

---

[3] "New Orientation Proposed for the Teaching of the Social Sciences in the Elementary School", Ministry of Education, Quebec, 1971, p. 4.

an intellectual attitude that makes the child interested in learning about his environment and gives him a technique for independent learning. Lastly, the new orientation . . . helps the child to progressively develop a sense of time and space and to gradually learn about human life in all its complexity.[4]

A working paper on the Teaching of Elementary Social Studies, published by the Nova Scotia Department of Education in 1975, proposes a multi-disciplinary curriculum. Concepts and goals selected from geography, sociology, history, economics, anthropology and political science are utilised at each stage of the programme as it moves out in a logical sequence through the grade levels : Year I—Self, Home, Neighbourhood, School; Year II—Children and Families; Year III—Children and Communities; Year IV—Communities and Region; Year IV—Man in His Changing Environments; Year VI— Canada and the World's People; Year VII—The Atlantic Provinces.

One of the most recent and thoroughly articulated programmes in Canada is the 1978 Alberta Social Studies Curriculum, Interim Edition, which was made available for use in Alberta schools as an alternative programme in the Fall of that year. The curriculum was designed "to ensure that all students achieve a basic foundation of value, knowledge, and skill objectives" by means of a logical sequence of learning experiences through the elementary and secondary grades.

The content of the Revised Curriculum consists mainly of topics, three per grade being designated for Grades One to Ten, and two per grade for Grades Eleven and Twelve. In conjunction with each topic, a "General Social Studies Issue" has also been identified for study.

The topics have been selected according to certain criteria, including the stages of development and interests of students, a balance of local/Canadian/global studies, and a broad spectrum of Canadian studies. Regarding the latter criterion, the 1978 Curriculum acknowledges the concern of most Canadians for students to become more knowledgeable about their own country. Accordingly the allocation of time to "Canadian Studies" has been increased substantially, amounting to about 50% of the total prescribed programme. In Grades 1-3, students are introduced to the general features of Canadian culture, to urban and rural lifestyles; and to the concepts of "passage of time" and "change" in their own local communities. In Grades 4-6 the curriculum comprises the following content-areas : the "roots" of Albertans, lifestyles in major eras in Alberta's history, Alberta's physical features and natural resources; events surrounding the creation of Alberta as a province; Alberta's place in Canada; Canada's cultural history to the settlement of Western Canada; Canada's demographic and economic regions; and political processes at the local, provincial and national levels.

---

4   "The Human Sciences in the Elementary School", Booklet No. 2, p. 11.

The value-objectives of the Curriculum are three-fold : growth in understanding of human values; development of positive attitudes towards self, other people, and man's environment; and development of competences in processes of moral reasoning and value analysis.

The skill-objectives include four categories, namely skills for (a) resolving value conflict; (B) building knowledge; (c) interacting purposefully with other people; and (d) applying what is learned.

The Curriculum is interdisciplinary rather than multidisciplinary. Thirteen concepts have been identified to furnish the organizing ideas from which the knowledge base of the programme is developed. The concepts have been selected according to the following criteria : they are fundamental concepts in either history, geography or the social sciences, and have application in a number of disciplines; and they are appropriate to the goal of citizenship—development that underlies the Alberta Social Studies Curriculum.

The thirteen concepts—human needs, identity, value, perspective, inquiry, interaction, influence, social change, adjustment, environment, institution, power and resources—are grouped in three broad categories, "Man as Individual", "Man's Processes" and "Man's Systems". For each grade level a concept is taken from each of the three categories for examination and development. Care is taken to ensure that development of all thirteen concepts occurs at each division—primary, upper elementary, junior and senior high school levels. In this manner the content of the social studies programme is introduced and developed in a spiral manner throughout the grades.[5]

In all the revised elementary social studies curricula introduced in Canada since the mid-1960's, geography has been acknowledged as an essential component, and in a number of provinces, particularly British Columbia, Manitoba and the Maritimes, it has been upgraded and strengthened. Trends towards fieldwork and inductive teaching, together with ampler provision of varied and up-to-date audio-visual materials, have become widely established.

On the basis of experience and research it is possible to characterise the kind of geography teaching that can and should be taking place in elementary schools today. First, it should be consistent with the philosophy of social studies exemplified in the various new curricula now in general use. Geography is taught not as a separate time-tabled subject but as part of topics and projects in social studies. It is sometimes the starting-point of a topic; at other times it will arise as part of a topic which had its beginnings in another discipline. The key to good teaching then, is flexibility, the ability to maintain an element of structure and at the same time capitalize on the day-to-day interests of the children, which are not confined within any disciplinary frame-work.

Second, the methods of teaching geography should take account of the findings of educational psychology and be in accord with modern practice in other subjects such as elementary science and mathematics. The views of Piaget have been particularly influential, resulting in the adoption of active rather than passive learning, with the teaching based on the children's own experience. The characteristics of children's thinking at the intuitive and concrete operational stages should be clearly understood, and their implications applied to the teaching of geographical concepts and skills, for example, in mapwork.

Finally, the geography taught should reflect its essential nature and be in tune with modern thinking in the subject. It is useful to keep in mind the existence of the four basic traditions in geography: the earth science, manland, area studies, and spatial traditions.[6] While all four have continuing relevance to teaching as well as to research, the spatial tradition is the one which has been most recently emphasized. A change of emphasis has also taken place with regard to the learning of facts. In the past, geography largely consisted of accumulating data of various kinds about places. Within the last twenty years, however, an attempt has been made to identify the basic ideas that lie at the heart of the discipline, and the focus of attention has been on spatial concepts, such as distance, direction, scale, spatial location, distribution, change, movement and relationship. It is these key concepts, comprising the foundation of the subject, that should be taught in the elementary school rather than numerous simple facts about places. In line with the theories of Bruner, geographers believe that by teaching the "big ideas" constituting the structure of the subject in progressively more complex forms, the children can ultimately attain a sound grasp of the discipline. Facts can be fascinating and they need to be learned, but it is better for them to be acquired through the understanding of concepts rather than as ends in themselves. Recent developments in applied geography at the professional level have highlighted the role of values in public decision-making, for example, concerning land-use, suggesting that geographical education should move in the direction of greater emphasis on values.[7]

There are two main approaches to geography teaching: one is real-life experience through field study in the community, and the second is vacarious experience where reality is simulated through the use of a wide range of materials and learning activities in the classroom.

The importance of local field-study can hardly be overemphasized: "a single period devoted to intelligent study of the school surroundings will promote more real understanding than the

---

[6]   William D. PATTISON, "The Four Traditions in Geography", Professional Paper No. 25, National Council for Geographic Education (May, 1964).

[7]   R. J. AMBROSE, "New Developments in Geography", in Rex WALFORD (ed.), New Directions in Geography Teaching (London; Longman, 1973), pp. 79-81.

memorization of a whole book full of ready-made generalizations about the area in question".[8]

Young children at the kindergarten and earliest grade levels are interested more or less in everything with which they make contact; their curiosity is unbounded, their questions are endless. They enjoy observing, collecting, drawing and modelling, exploring, and listening to stories. At this stage they receive their geographical training incidentally, through the activities involved in studying a series of centres of interest or topics based on first-hand observation in the school locality. The teacher should select topics that are likely to prove fruitful from a geographical standpoint. Ideally the interest should come from the child. The teacher will therefore contrive to bring her pupils into contact with any pre-chosen situation just when something likely to catch their interest is happening, e.g. a visit to a local orchard at harvesting-time. Places where there is usually plenty of activity —railway stations, goods yards, factories, quarries, town or country markets—interest children and provide plenty of "raw material" for subsequent conversation, drawing and modelling. Such visits also provide the children with the opportunity to learn, by direct questionning, something about the work of the people they have observed. From their investigations the children will gradually begin to form their first notions of the meaning of geographical concepts like "transport", "industry", "communications", and if there is a convenient stream nearby, perhaps also "deposition", "erosion", etc. They will not be taught definitions and may not even hear such terms mentioned, but they will be receiving the necessary foundations for a proper understanding of these terms when they meet them later.

Observations of weather phenomena should also be encouraged, not necessarily for the purpose of keeping a daily record—that can come later, when wind directions, clouds, rainfall amounts and temperatures can be systematically studied—but in order to relate weather and seasonal changes with changes in clothing and occupations throughout the year, and noting their influence on transport, vegetation, animal life and agricultural activities.

Experiments with shadows cast by a vertical stick at mid-day are valuable for demonstrating the seasonal variation in the altitude of the sun, and also provide a suitable practical method of introducing the children to compass directions.

Geography is correlated closely with Nature Study in the primary grades; the knowledge gained from making direct observations of plant and animal life, including the collection of specimens of plants, wild flowers, leaves of trees, etc. forms the best possible foundation for later studies involving natural vegetation and agriculture. The effects of altitude, aspect, soils and seasonal changes on plant life can best be brought home to the child by this means.

---

[8]   D. M. TOMKINS, *Discovering Our Land—Teacher's Guide*, (Toronto: W.J. Gage Ltd., 1966), p. 10.

Direct observation of farming processes in the different seasons of the year is also very important. Rural schools obviously have an advantage over town schools as far as the observation of natural phenomena is concerned. Yet the urban teacher is not entirely without resources in this respect: she can always make use of local parks and gardens. Possible lines of investigation might include: "Is the land in the park level, rolling or hilly? What are the main types of soil? What kinds of vegetation grow in the park? Is any of this natural? Which was hand-planted?"

For studying agriculture processes, however, it would be necessary to organize visits to a farm. However sophisticated and globally-minded today's city children may be, they are often remarkably parochial in their knowledge: comparatively few really understand the meaning of such a universal and fundamental process as ploughing, for instance, because the majority of them have never seen a plough at work. Similarly, many city children have never seen cows being milked by either traditional or modern mechanical methods. It would be difficult to over-emphasize the value to urban children of such visits which, ideally, should be made three or four times, at different seasons of the year, to cover the major farming operations.

The world for most Canadian children today is a highly urbanized one with all the attendant problems of an urban society. Every child will be faced with the responsibility for making decisions about this world when he or she matures and becomes a voter within our democratic system. The importance of the early years in moulding a child's future is a compelling reason for an early introduction to urban studies. There is much of value that can be studied in the immediate neighbourhood of any town or city school. It is not necessary to hire buses or plan far-away excursions in order to provide field experiences for children. A one-hour walk in the vicinity of the school can develop many skills and yield much data for subsequent classroom use.

In this connection, a host of useful ideas for the classroom teacher is provided in *Primary Five to Nine*, a resource book prepared after extensive research and collaborative effort under the auspices of "Project Canada West" and the Canada Studies Foundation.

Included in the resource book is an account of a study of a school block which was conducted in a Canadian school, involving group studies of various aspects of the urban environment: houses and yards; sounds; nature; traffic, roads and signs; people's and services. A wide variety of skills was employed: observing, classifying, making inferences, and drawing conclusions. Methods of recording the children's observations took the form of drawing, painting, writing individual and class books, graphing, mapping, measuring, tape-recording, photographing and interviewing. Knowledge—outcomes of the study included a greater awareness of both the physical and man-made features of the block and an introduction to the concept of land-use. The children also developed attitudes of increased confidence in carrying out independent enquiry and greater awareness of the interests and values of other people.[9]

Shopping is a very fruitful area for field study: it is part of all our daily lives, and stores are a prominent feature of the urban landscape. There are well-developed geographic theories of retailing activity, which presuppose that the urban retail scene is orderly and patterned. Older elementary school children can be led to discover the patterns underlying shopping habits and retail activity. The existence of such a theoretical framework shows how the study of geography has moved from a purely descriptive, information-gathering exercise to one that is conceptually oriented. The framework suggests dozens of questions that can guide pupils in observing retail patterns in their own communities.[10]

It has often been said that maps are the geographer's chief tool, and that no sound geographical education can take place without their regular use. Attracted by their colourfulness, children seem interested in maps at a very early age, and because of this interest there has been a tendency in the past to use maps too early, before children are capable of understanding them. Maps are a complex form of symbolic representation, and skill in understanding and using them is acquired only very gradually through careful, systematic teaching. In a summary of the research in North America on children's ability to read maps, H. A. Rushdooney states, "Children's errors or misconceptions were more a lack of systematic teaching than children's ability to read maps".[11]

To ensure that map-work is a meaningful, enjoyable experience for the child, it should be taught not in isolation but as an integral if often incidental part of the whole Social Studies program. The emphasis should be on "learning by doing", and the map must always be seen to have a purpose and use beyond itself. The main objective is to gradually develop in the children "map consciousness", that easy familiarity with maps which is achieved when they have come to regard them as a natural medium of expression. This can be done through accustoming the children to make maps for themselves and use them.

The first maps should be plans of what they can see at the time, e.g. maps of the classroom to show the way the children go to their seats, or to show the position of the radiators, etc. followed at a later stage by maps to show the way to the classroom from the principal's

[9] P. HARPER et al., Project Five to Nine (Toronto: MacMillan Company of Canada Ltd., 1975), pp. 32-38.

[10] Details of field-work activities in the geography of retailing are succinctly outlined in G. S. TOMKINS, "Field Studies Right Under Our Noses", in Monday Morning, September 1968, pp. 40-41.

[11] Haig A. RUSHDOONEY, "A Child's Ability to Read Maps: Summary of the Research", Journal of Geography, Vol. XVII (1968), pp. 213-222. See also Wayne .. HERMAN, Jr. Current Research in Elementary School Social Studies (Toronto: Collier-Macmillan, 1969), pp. 405-433.

office, or the way from the school to the local post office. If the area represented by the map is gradually increased and the children are always required to draw their maps on sheets of a uniform size they will begin to grasp the concept of scale, although the need for accurate drawing to a pre-determined scale will not arise until later.

In making this series of roughly-drawn maps, certain principles emerge which are common to all map-making. For example, there is a particular purpose for each map. Every one of them can be labelled; "A map to show... etc." This is a good habit to acquire from the beginning, for one of the main faults of many maps made later on in school life is that they try to show too much and end up by showing nothing well. It should be remembered that very soon the children will be asked to read what the maps have to tell them, and this is not easy to do if they are overloaded with a heterogeneous collection of facts. It is far better to make a series of maps, each with a limited but clearly defined purpose expressed in the title, than to make one which is over-ambitious and which fails as a result.

Another basic principle is that of "key" or "legend". Many different symbols and representations constitute the language of the map through which it tells its story, and this language must be properly understood when the map is read. It is more likely to be understood when children have been accustomed to using the language in making their own maps. They should also understand that other people may use the same map and to them the language may not be so clear; therefore the map language must always be explained in the form of a legend or key which makes the message of the map clear to all who may need to use it. Children should be trained to supply a key with every map that uses any form of representation, and they should regard a map as incomplete without it.

When the children are able to make a reasonable attempt at showing the lay-out of the local streets and roads they should be introduced to their first real map—a large-scale map of the immediate area. It is sometimes possible to obtain maps on a scale of 1:2400 or 1:4800 from municipal planning authorities in Canada, and these are ideal for use with young children. If possible, sufficient copies of the maps should be available to allow study by small groups. The children will be quite capable of understanding the map; they will enjoy identifying and colouring their own homes, and locating the local landmarks, buildings and roads which they know so well. Air photographs of the locality, if obtainable, are also valuable in this connection.

From using these maps in their field studies the children will realize the use of the cardinal points and the importance of orientating the map correctly. At the Grade 5 and 6 levels they can be gradually introduced to the 1:25,000 and 1:50,000 sheets of their own locality in the National Topographic Series. Simplified sections might be used at first, then the maps themselves can be used outdoors. The map symbols can be progressively learned through recognition of relevant objects in the field. Concomitant activities may include sketching traffic census work, street transects and land-use study.[12]

The globe, as the most realistic representation of the earth as a whole, has a unique place, and as a model and a map it will gradually come to have increasing meaning. Its use from grade to grade, combined with observations which the pupils make of such phenomena as sun shadows, the varying length of day and night, and the more obvious movements of the moon and planets, will help in leading to a conception of the earth as a spinning sphere revolving around the sun, and to some of the implications of this conception.[13]

However important may be the local area in geographical study, it is a fact that nowadays the wider world beyond one's own neighbourhood and community is brought daily into the home via radio and television. As soon as the child expresses an interest in it, the teacher may introduce into the classroom topics and materials to satisfy his curiosity. Clearly most of the material for such work will have to be second-hand, that is, it must be experienced through books, pictures, and other media which are a substitute for actual visits.

Short of the real thing, pictures are the best substitute for reality that we can find. The pictures selected for classroom use should be sharp and clear, rich in geographic content, and they should lend themselves to questioning. They should normally form an integral part of the lesson, rather than a separate item of illustration at the end of it. Research shows that it is best not to use too many pictures—no more than eight should be used in a given lesson, and intensive study of even fewer is beneficial. Research has shown that children need a great deal of guidance in appreciating scale, and that they tend to focus on minute and often unimportant detail.[14]

Various stages in teaching may be followed according to maturity of the children and the purposes of the particular study. At the simplest level, pupils may be asked to name or enumerate items in a picture. This may be done for the purpose of building vocabulary, or perhaps making comparisons with the home environment. In the second stage, the pupil describes and explains what he sees: for example, from the type of vegetation seen in the picture he may attempt to infer the possible climate of the area. In the stage of interpretation, a more systematic attempt is made to derive geographical relationships.

In training children to make the best use of pictures, such terms as "foreground", "middle-ground" and "background" should become familiar. Pictures can be analyzed from the viewpoint of the

---

[12] For detailed examples, see Geography In Primary Schools, (Sheffield: Geographical Association, [n.d.], pp. 30-38.

[13] For an excellent discussion of the use of the globe, see Olive GARNETT, Fundamentals in School Geography, 3rd ed. revised (London: George Harrap, 1965), ch. V.

[14] M. LONG and B.S. ROBERSON, Teaching Geography (Toronto: Bellhaven House Ltd., 1967), Ch. 5.

natural and cultural landscape—topography, climate, soils, vegetation, natural resources, occupations, population density and standards of living.

Picture-study forms an important element in the elementary Social Studies programme in Canada today, and a variety of excellent picture-sets is made available for schools in an increasing number of provinces.

Filmstrips, slides and films are being used to a greater extent than formerly. Projected still pictures, such as filmstrip frames and slides, have the advantage that they are large and clear enough to be studied simultaneously by a large class. Eight or ten frames from a filmstrip, or the same number of slides, can provide enough material for discussion to initiate a substantial project.

Ciné films have an immediacy and realism that far surpass that of projected still film. The fact that more 16mm film is in colour gives it an added attraction. The ideal situation is for every elementary school to possess a 16mm film projector and suitable black-out materials.

Radio and television broadcasts can also induce the feeling of having experienced something real. In particular, they can introduce children to the music, art and crafts of other people, and so contribute to a balanced picture of the region.

Specimens and collections of rocks, fossils, minerals, and human artifacts have a similar usefulness. They can often be used to illustrate what has been already discussed, but even more often as a starting point for investigation.

One of the best and most widely used method of bringing the outside world into the elementary classroom is the sample or "case study". With children in the earlier grades, this can be done by means of a story about the life of a real child and his or her family living in a real community in some other region or country. At Grade 5, 6 and above, it is valuable to lead on to the study of a town, village, city, or rural district, using as much first-hand material as possible. This should approximate to the material the children will have collected about their own locality—statistics of weather, graphs, large-scale maps, travellers' descriptions, photographs, slides and films. The aim is to build up a vivid, detailed and realistic picture of the topic under consideration. The emphasis is on real people in a real place, following a round of existence similar to, while often in other ways different from, that of the children and their families here at home.

The sample or case study is what the name says—a *study*, implying that the students must be actively involved in the use and exploration of the various materials, and be guided skilfully to the desired conclusions. In deploying the source materials, questions should be framed which will point to important and relevant facts, require answers to be inferred from evidence, encourage the students to make intelligent guesses, permit contrast and comparison with the local area and lead to generalizations.

Geographers today are making increasing use of quantitative data, for which they require to use statistical techniques. Some of these techniques have found their way into elementary mathematics and science teaching recently in Britain. Their application to geography is illustrated in a series of elementary textbooks, called *New Ways in Geography* by J. P. Cole and J. H. Beynon. According to the authors, the aims and characteristics of the series include the following:

> 1. The series is intended to make available in a very diluted form for younger children some of the techniques and concepts currently found in University geography. The following are emphasized: spatial relationships, the handling of relationships, problem-solving, and the application of mathematics and statistics. 2. While the relevance of the local area to the study of geography is appreciated, it is felt that a world view is also worth cultivating. A child of ten can now watch a man walking on the moon, and can see the planet Earth from outer space. Surely that child's concept of distance and space is superior to the concepts adults had several decades ago when space travel was beyond the realms of possibility. 3. The exercises... are intended to make children participate in the problems they are solving and to make decisions about geographical situations such as finding the shortest journey or locating a steel works. 4. The experience of the children is drawn on as far as possible. There are exercises on travel to school, relatives, holiday resorts. They are asked to note what they pick up on radio, television, and in the newspapers. They should take note of the place of origin of the various things they consume.[15]

These books contain a number of role-playing games, in which the participants are required to make decisions on the basis of a given body of data. The games provide a framework within which children are easily motivated and can actively participate to find out more about geography. However, they need to be integrated into conventional approaches, otherwise they would be in danger of being regarded and used merely as gimmicks.

Finally, despite the wide variety of other aids, books remain an essential source of information and delight. For very young children, folk-tales provide an introduction to the people and traditions of other lands. To older children, books of travel and discovery have a strong appeal, especially if a sense of adventure is conveyed; and they often provide excellent detailed descriptions. A wide variety of these and of such reference materials as encyclopedias, gazeteers and geographical magazines should always be available. It is possible also to increase the range of the children's reference library by buying a variety of books, in small sets or in individual copies, instead of purchasing for class teaching one or two graduated series. In all cases it is worth paying attention to production as well as to content. Language and size of print should be suitable, format must be attractive and pictures

---

[15]   J. P. COLE and N. J. BEYNON, *New Ways in Geography* (Book 3)—*A Guide for Teachers* (Oxford: Basil Blackwell, 1968), p. 3.

so selected that they are aesthetically pleasing as well as geographically significant.

The difficulty in geography-teaching today is never that of finding interesting material, but rather that of selecting the most effective aids from the wealth available. The quality of Social Studies education depends not chiefly on equipment, facilities or materials, but on the quality of the individual teachers. Particularly heavy demands are made on teachers of geography. They need to have a firm grasp of the basic principles of the subject, and a sound body of knowledge. They need to be well read and to adopt all possible means to keep themselves up-to-date. Above all they should be persons of wide interests, for much of the success of their teaching depends on the ability to handle material from related subjects, and to integrate it and distil (1) it for the benefit of their pupils. If teachers today can rise to the challenge, no subject in the curriculum will be more exciting and rewarding than Social Studies.

GEOGRAPHY AND THE ENVIRONMENT

JOHN TOWLER
Renison College, University of Waterloo.

For one reason or another, Geography has suffered from periodic attempts to define it, redefine it, identify its most pervasive goals, determine its historical parameters or forecast its future directions. Indeed, it can be argued that there has already been far too much of this sort of thing in the past and there is little need or interest in continuing with these introspective bloodlettings. Yet here again is another article dealing with geography and what it is or should be. However, what follows is *not* merely another dry discourse on what it is or is not, rather it is an attempt to point out that environmental studies, a new area of the school curriculum, is gaining increased attention and that a group of adherents is either duplicating areas of interest which have normally resided with geographers in the past, or are usurping those areas because of the disinterest and/or lack of action on the part of geograpers. Unless one is a geographer, (and perhaps even if this is the case), a typical response to this state of affairs seems to be, "So what !" One should really care less about who teaches environmental studies, environmental education or whatever it is called provided that it is taught and taught effectively. However, a rather good case can and should be made for geograpers taking a hand in this since they are one of the groups best equipped by training and experience to do the most effective job. In addition, they have (or should have) had a long standing interest in this subject area. Whether this sort of squatters rights to the subject means anything or not remains to be seen. Certainly it should go without saying that if the geographers are not prepared to do an effective job in environmental education, they should get out of the way and leave the field to others.

For at least the past ten years, both academic geographers and geographic educators (those who are more interested in the teaching of geography) have been discussing the growing area of environmental studies and its relationship to geography. Sometimes, but not always, these two groups talk to each other. Usually though, they are rather insulated and in North America are represented by such separate organization as the Canadian Association of Geographers and the National Association for Geographic Education. A similar pattern holds true for the USA and in the UK where one finds two groups represented by such bodies as the Institute of British Geographers and the Town and Country Planning Association.

The teaching geographers have more or less got on with the job of introducing environmental education into their courses and sphere of interest with a minimum of attention as to where and how it fits within the parent discipline. Writers like Swan (1971) have encouraged geographers to deal with environmental issues, but there has been nothing like the quantity and quality of pieces produced by the academics. This is probably as it should be, except for the fact that this attention from the academics is in danger of being too little too late to enable geography to assume a place of influence and leadership in the field. Geographers have established a sort of foot-hold in environmental studies and there are geographers who are making significant contributions, but unless the profession as a whole increases its awareness and commitment, both geography and environmental studies will be the poorer as a result.

Hare (1969) was one of the first geographers to raise the issue of geography's role in environmental studies. As he pointed out, even at the turn of the century, geographers were concerned with environmental issues. This was reflected in the works of Semple, (1911), Barrows (1923) who emphasized geography's interest in man-land relationships. For one reason or another, this interest seemed to flag after the 1930's and was replaced by a series of emphases as geography bent to whatever wind was blowing at the time. Hence we have seen a number of paradigm changes including wholism, regionalism, dualism, the quantitative era and now environmentalism. However, even with regard to the latter, geographers are late in becoming involved. Perhaps Hare (1969, p. 53) was correct when he commented, "sometimes I think that geography as a science deliberately stays out of phase with the climate of the times". Whether this is the case or not remains to be seen, but it is clear that geography is losing ground in this area at least with regard to what is happening in the schools in this country. Hare suggested in 1969 that geographers had to look over their shoulder to make sure they were not being left behind. If anything, the situation has worsened in the last ten years and the gap has widened.

Hare's original article invoked a number of responses and a healthy degree of attention. Clayton (1970) felt that the situation in the UK was worse than Hare stated and suggested that geography does not contribute very easily to the environmental sciences. However, this certainly need not be the case. Geography has always claimed to be and acted as an integrating discipline. Geographers have traditionally dealt with the interrelationships of all phenomena and have recognized that nothing exists in isolation. Von Humboldt and Ritter expressed this central concept of geography as "zusammenhang" and stressed the need to understand things in context. The difficulty lies in the fact that geographers have lost sight of this central theme and as Goodey (1970, 1971), Wheeler (1971) and other have suggested, geography has failed to speak to the issue of improving environmental conditions and has not offered great leadership to those concerned with the future of our environment. Goodey (1971) called for a radically new framework for geography and stated that the environmental crisis demands a response from geographers. O'Riordan (1970) claimed that this was already taking place at least in Canada and that a new spirit of academic community has developed with the geographer acting as a synthesizer with others in related fields. Undoubtedly, this is true to some extent and we have already witnessed the creation of institutes of environmental studies like that at the University of Toronto and the creation of faculties of environmental studies including departments of geography such as the one at the University of Waterloo. Yet, geography seems to confine itself to the role of a lesser member of the interdisciplinary team. A rather good case can be made that it ought to be exercising more leadership in these ventures. It has the background, experience and methodology to act as *the* integrating element if it so desired.

In the final analysis, it is of little consequence how it occurs or who assumes the major role as long as society benefits from increased attention to environmental matters and that a generation of decision makers are prepared to manage their world responsibly. Yet we know from the studies of Lowenthal (1967), Saarinen (1969) and others that decisions about the environment are made on the basis of how people perceive the environment and that this may differ greatly from the way it actually is. Since geographers have always claimed that the elements comprising these relationships are the meat of their discipline and that they are singularly able to examine and understand them, it follows that geographers are central and not peripheral to environmental studies. Perhaps this is not a serious problem at the university level where interdisciplinary teams and departments already exist, and where the boundaries between the disciplines have already become quite blurred. The major problem arises within the elementary and secondary school systems where environmental studies is being taught but in the majority of case, neither by an interdisciplinary team nor by geographers. The usual pattern is one in which environmental man-land relationships are being taught by the science teacher or by generalists who have little or no geographical background. The situation is more severe in the faculties of colleges of education in Canada where the majority of the instructors teaching students how to teach environmental studies have backgrounds in science or education, but not geography. If this pattern continues and geographers close their minds to it, geography's place and importance in the school curricula will continue to decline and the gap will be filled by disciplines whose members are more aware and more active. Aside from the obvious ramifications for geography as a discipline and its ability to remain relevant and attract students, the continuation of this pattern of inadequate involvement renders a disservice to environmental studies which can and ought to profit from the expertise that geographers can bring.

I.—INTERNATIONAL PROGRAMME IN ENVIRONMENTAL EDUCATION

For the past several years, there have been great efforts on an international scale to focus attention on environmental education and to further national efforts in this area. Recognizing the world-wide need for education about our environment and the necessity to raise the environmental literacy of people at all ages, UNESCO (United National Education, Scientific and Cultural Organization) hosted an United Nations Conference on the Human Environment in Stockholm in 1972. Arising from that conference was the creation of the United Nations Environment Programme (UNEP). This body was developed to establish an international programme in environmental education, interdisciplinary in approach, in school and out-of-school, encompassing all levels of education and directed towards the general public. In particular attention was focused on the ordinary citizen living in rural and urban areas, youth and adult alike with a view to educating him to the simple steps he might take to manage his environment. Among the activities which followed from the Stockholm conference were the creation of a newsletter, CONNECT, which serves as the international communications network for some 10,000 individuals and institutions around the world.[1] Another important venture was an international survey done in 1975 of the needs of priorities in environmental education of the 136 member states of the UN. With a return rate of 82%, the resultant data were used to prepare the world's first overview of what the various countries felt were their most pressing environmental education problems[2]

The Stockholm conference was followed in 1975 by an international workshop for experts in the field. This was held in Belgrade, Yugoslavia in October of that year and was followed by a series of regional and subregional meetings in every major area of the world. At the same time, eighteen pilot projects in various world regions were underway testing out new methodologies, curricula, materials and programmes. All of these activities were part of the preparations leading to the culminating activity which was the Intergovernmental Conference on Environmental Education which was held in Tbilisi, USSR, October 1977. Canada has been represented at each of these meetings and has taken an active part in each of the activites. Unfortunately much of this has gone unrecognized at home.

Obviously, there has been a great deal of attention and action surrounding the field of environmental education. It clearly exists in

---

[1] CONNECT is available free of charge by writing to UNESCO, 7 place de Fontenoy, Paris, France, and requesting that one's name be added to their mailing list. The newsletter contains information about the environmental education activities of member countries.

[2] The final report is entitled *Needs and Priorities in Environmental Education: An International Survey.*, (Paris: UNESCO/ENVED 6), 1977.

almost every country of the world and is growing in strength and importance. It has long passed the fad and bandwagon stage of popularity and has given rise to a subject area which is rapidly developing a body of knowledge, authoritative research, methods, materials and advanced degrees. However, because of its newness and the problem of where and how to interject it into the school curriculum, it has not developed a clear and separate identity, at least in the minds of some educators and professionals in o ther fields such as geography. This seems to be a particularly serious problem in Canada where one finds a number of excellent programmes underway, but a total lack of any consistent policy, direction, priorities or even a communications network among those involved.

II.—GEOGRAPHY AND ENVIRONMENTAL EDUCATION IN CANADIAN SCHOOLS

Due in part to the absence of a Federal Office of Education, geographic and environmental education varies greatly from Province to Province with little overall direction or consensus regarding content and emphasis. In spite of this, surveys by Rioux (1973) and Davis (1976) have shown that some form of environmental education is being taught in the schools of every province. There is great variation, ranging from provincially required courses like those in Ontario, to courses in the process of development such as those in Quebec and the Maritimes. The point is that environmental education (E.E.) has arrived in the schools but that it is not being treated as a separate subject pushing some other discipline out of the curriculum. Rather, it is being integrated into the existing curriculum in several ways. In most cases, this is occurring as a new emphasis in traditional disciplines, the addition of new units of study to existing courses or the blending of several disciplines to make a new area of study. Hence one may find the traditional general science course with a new focus on environmental topics and in some cases, even being renamed as "environmental science". In other instances, units on urban planning, waste water management, ecosystems, etc., have been interjected into geography, social studies, science, biology and similar courses. In some cases (like that of Ontario), one finds that the areas of science, social studies and health have been combined to create a new subject area called "environment studies" where the overall emphasis is clearly on the environment.

These are exciting and interesting developments, but in almost every case, they impinge on some facet of what was once the domain of geography. Geographic content has been diluted over the years and the process has merely been accelerated by the interest in environmental concerns. This is a rather perverse result for a discipline that claims to be already inexoribly involved with the environment. But the picture is clear. What once was physical geography, became earth science (Towler and DeVito, 1970). What once was the separate subject of geography, became one part of the subject known as social studies. Now, at least in Ontario, this has been subsumed within environmental studies. Perhaps the geographers have got what they deserved by their lack of attention and interest. However, E.E. does not deserve this treatment from them and suffers from their absence.

III. — CANADIAN PROBLEMS, NEEDS AND PRIORITIES

There are an unlimited number of ways in which geographers can make significant contributions to their own discipline and to E.E. One way of approaching this is to identify the problems, needs and priorities, then to take action in one of these directions.

There have been at least four studies of E.E. in Canada in recent years. The first by Rioux (1973) pointed out the absence of any consistent set of national objectives, policies, research efforts or feedback mechanisms. Rioux lamented the lack of support from departments of education, provincial and resource management agencies or the federal government and suggested that E.E. was severely hampered by this inattention.

A second survey of the Canadian scene was done by Davis (1976) who gathered data on policies and school practices from each of the provincial departments of education. This study revealed that while each province claimed to have an interest in E.E. and reported the presence of some courses, none had developed a specific policy regarding E.E. However, in almost every province, various committees were meeting and some form of E.E. was being taught in the schools with the approval of the provincial and local authorities.

A third study was initiated by UNESCO/UNEP in 1975 as part of their survey of global needs and priorities. Canada was one of the countries surveyed at that time and submitted data concerning its needs and priorities regarding legislation, programs, personnel, instructional materials and organizations and associations in E.E. The data were later analysed according to the levels of pre-school, primary, secondary and tertiary education plus education for out-of-school youth and adults.

The results indicated that our greatest need was for personnel trained to teach E.E. particularly at the tertiary level of education and also at the pre-school, primary and secondary levels as well as education for out-of-school youth. Our national priorities were identified according to the following ranking.

1. Adult education.
2. Primary education.
3. Secondary, tertiary and out-of-school youth education.
4. Pre-school education.

The results of the UNESCO/UNEP survey must be interpreted with some care because of the unusual manner in which the Canadian data were collected. In the absence of a central office or national department of education, the questionnaires used in the study were sent to a variety of provincial offices, agencies and individuals. Their responses were used as the raw data from which the Canadian situation was extrapolated. However, regardless of the rigour of the sampling method, the results seem quite consistent with the North American scene and parallel the situation in the U.S.A.

A more recent study was conducted in 1979 by Towler (Towler, 1979) in which each of the 48 faculties of education and teacher training institutions in Canada were surveyed in an attempt to determine the state of the art in E.E. Based on a response rate of 85% the data indicated that fewer than 50% of the institutions offer a course in teaching environmental education. Hence in the 1977-78 school year, only 1514 prospective Canadian teachers received instruction in teaching E.E. While a higher proportion of the institutions offered courses dealing with ecological content (more than 62%) there were 300 fewer students enrolled in such courses. Thus it would appear that very few teachers are being taught how to teach E.E. and even fewer are receiving an adequate background in the content. If this is Canada's best effort to meet her number one priority for more trained personnel, we have a long way to go.

Another area of personnel weakness revealed by the Towler study concerns the background of the faculty who are teaching E.E. methods. Only 10% of the institutions have a faculty who have prior teaching experience in E.E. and few, if any of these have degrees in the field. This is not as alarming as it may first appear given the newness of the field and the comparatively recent creation of tertiary programs in E.E. Nevertheless, it seems that faculty members with backgrounds in general science and/or education are the ones most likely to be teaching prospective teachers how to teach E.E. In addition, these faculty members are the same ones who are most likely to be involved in developing programs for use in the school systems.

Other data revealed by this study which should be of particular interest to geographers is that 97% of the respondents felt that E.E. ought to be integrated into the science area in the elementary and secondary schools and fewer than 28% felt it should be part of a geography course. The major needs identified by the respondents were ranked as follows:

1. Communication among environmental educators.
2. Funding.
3. Research and materials for teachers.
4. Canadian content in materials.
5. Teaching materials and equipment.
6. Texts for students.

The lack of communication is a particularly severe one in Canada where at present there is no national or inter-provincial body concerned with E.E. serving the needs of those working in the area. Two examples will suffice to point out the magnitude of this problem.

The UNESCO effort in E.E. culminated in a world conference held in Tbilisi in October of 1977. In the interim, nearly every other major country in the world has held a post-Tbilisi task force meeting to address its national E.E. needs. Canada has yet to hold such a meeting and efforts to involve the federal or provincial governments in such a venture have proved fruitless. The results of this lack of national attention to E.E. and our inability to communicate with each other has resulted in a situation in which one finds that while each Canadian province claims to have some form of policy regarding the need for E.E., 9% of our teacher-training institutions indicated that they do not offer teacher education in E.E. and justify this with the claim that there has been no demand from local school boards for them to do so! One can only conclude that these boards and institutions are either unaward or uninterested in the educational efforts of the rest of the country.

CONCLUSIONS AND SUGGESTIONS FOR FUTURE ACTION

It is clear that geographers have had and will continue to have an interest and involvement in matters pertaining to the environment. Their contributions to this area have not been clearly defined nor have they been consistently effective. However, the educational systems in Canada are currently focusing their attention on programs and projects specifically pertaining to the environment. This has resulted in the creation of a number of needs which geograpers are particularly equipped to meet. Involvement in such ventures would prove profitable for both disciplines.

Geographers and their associations could render a valuable service to this country by supporting three important projects: the convening of a national task force on E.E.; the development of a communication network for those working in this field; and the development of a group of professionals who could assist authorities in applyint geographic knowledge to teaching about the environment. Ultimately, the first two of these needs will be met with or without geographers and in the final analysis, it may be unimportant whether these professionals involve themselves or not. However, if Canadian geographers will take the effort to follow their own traditions and contribute to environmental education, the results will be of great value both for geography and E.E.

BIBLIOGRAPHY

ALDRICH, J.L., et al., The Report of the North American Regional Seminar on Environmental Education (Columbus, Ohio: SMEAC, Ohio State University, 1977).

BALL, John M., et al., The Social Sciences and Geographic Education (New York: John Wiley and Sons, 1971).

BARROWS, H. H., "Geography as Human Ecology", *Annals of the Association of American Geographers*, 13 (1923), 1-14.

CLAYTON, Keith, "Environmental Science", *AREA*, 1 (1970), 5-6.

DAVIS, Jack, *Environmental Education in Canada—1976* (Toronto, Ont.: Ministry of Education, 1976).

GOODEY, Brian, "Environmental Studies and Interdisciplinary Research", *AREA*, 2 (1970), 16-18.

GOODEY, Brian, "Professional Barriers", *Bulletin of Environmental Education*, May 1971.

HARE, Kenneth, "Environment: Resuscitation of an Idea", *AREA*, 4 (1969), 52-55.

LOWENTHAL, D. (ed.), "Environmental Perception and Behaviour" University of Chicago, Dept. of Geography Research Paper 109, 1967.

O'RIORDAN, Timothy, "New Conservation and Geography", *AREA*, 4 (1970), 33-36.

RIOUX, J. C., *Environmental Education in Primary and Secondary Schools in Canada* (Ottawa: Environment Canada, 1973).

SAARINEN, T. F., *Perception of Environment* (Washington, D.C.: Association of American Geographers, Commission on College Geography, Resource Paper No. 5, 1969).

SEMPLE, E. C., *Influences of the Geographic Environment* (New York: Henry Holt, 1911).

SWAN, James, "The Challenge of Environmental Education", in *The Social Studies and Geographic Educations* (New York: John Wiley & Sons, 1971), 318-323.

TOWLER, John, and DEVITO, Alfred, "Geography in the Elementary School Isn't Dead, It's Fading", *School Science and Mathematics*, 70 (June 1970), 511-14.

TOWLER, John, "A Study of Environmental Education in Canadian Teacher Training Institutions" (mimeo), 1979.

TRANT, Anthony, *Environmental Education in the Age Group &-14 years in the European Community* (Dublin, Ireland: Trinity College, 1977).

UNESCO: IBE *World Trends in Environmental Education*, Bulletin of the International Bureau of Education, No. 200 (Paris: UNESCO, 1976).

UNESCO, *Needs and Priorities in Environmental Education: An International Survey* (Paris: UNESCO, 1977).

UNESCO, *Regional Meetings of Experts on Environmental Education, A Synthetic Report* (Paris: UNESCO, 1977).

UNESCO, *Trends in Environmental Education* (Paris: UNESCO, 1977).

UNESCO, *Needs and Priorities in Environmental Education: An International Survey* (Paris: UNESCO/UNEP. 6, 1977).

L'APPRENANT

THE LEARNER

MAPPING IN THE EARLY YEARS OF SCHOOLING

Dr. DENNIS MILBURN
University of British Columbia

The phrase "I could never draw a map" is very common among adults. If interpreted it could mean that those adults could not *construct* a map if there were a need to do so, or perhaps that they were unable to analyze a topographical map, or to reproduce a map of some part of the world from memory. Such activities will no doubt have been practised by adults during their own days in school and are still being practised by students today, with varied measures of success. The acquisition and understanding of map skills is a long and complex process, and depends on a progression of cognitive steps which need to be assimilated long before a child can be told to "copy that map from the board". In this chapter we shall attempt to look at the genesis of mapping techniques and note particularly how children approach mapping, rather than simply being taught about maps.

Many children's first introduction to maps is through world maps or national maps. This instructional method, however laudable, can often run counter to stages of child development. It is certainly not suggested that world maps be banished from classrooms in the early grades, but most children do not see mpas or globes as adults see them. For example, when a six year old looks at a classroom globe for the first time there is no reason to suppose, or know, that the blue areas on the globe represent seas or oceans. A very useful exercise for adults is to attempt to visualize a planetary globe with the seas as land masses and the land masses as seas. If this is done, those "shapes" which make up land masses on the globe become very different. When children are faced with a map of Canada, or a political map of a continent, with the provinces and countries mapped in different colours, then to children even up to the age of ten such maps may well represent only a pattern of colours rather than a distribution of spatial areas. Similarly adults may conceptualise that when they see a map on a television programme they could concentrate on the wrong colour. For example, on a map of South East Asia, if one concentrated by accident on the shape of the sea (which may be white) rather than on the long (and black) peninsula of Malaysia, then it would be very difficult to recognize the "simple shape" of the peninsula of Malaysia. Children may know nothing of the shapes of continents and can therefore look at the "wrong thing" and create a shape which they concentrate on and which may well be *their* perception of the map.

Children in kindergarten and first grade who are practising their first steps in mapping need to bring together, or codify, various concepts of space which they gradually build up into a network of co-ordinates. For example, a knowledge of what is vertical and what is horizontal, whether objects are to the right or to the left, and how things look from above, are all factors which children have to take into consideration and reinterpret as they draw any type of picture or plan which could loosely be described as a "map". To give an example of this, it is very common in children's drawings for them to mix up those objects which have horizontal and vertical features. Thus, objects may be drawn on their side or at an angle, depending on the child's point of view. When drawing a scene in the classroom the problem of transferring data from the right hand side of the classroom to the right hand side of a sheet of drawing paper can often pose difficulties, and particularly to children who are left handed. Objects can become scattered around the paper in incorrect positions.

We may also reflect on the difficulties young children have in drawing things from above. Piaget places the ability to do this around the age of eight.[1] We shall see later that this is a natural process of development (Figures 1 to 4). Children gradually assimilate the ability to move from a two dimensional view to a view from overhead. To

Figure 1

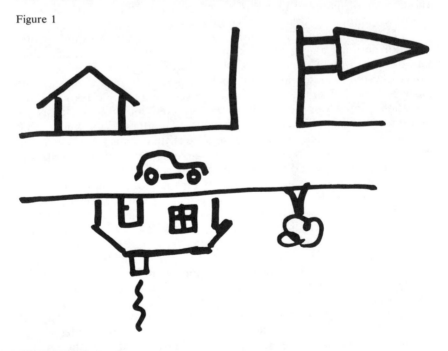

---

[1]   J. PIAGET & B. INHELDER, *The Child's concept of space* (Norton, 1967).

put it another way, children in the very early grades will find it almost impossible to conceptualize and draw anything "from above". If we further compound these approaches to mapping by stating that objects have to be spatially organized i.e. mapped according to their relative size and according to their relative distance one from another, then it is not difficult to envisage how complex a mental exercise this is.

Let us examine some aspects of a very common exercise which is given to children in the elementary school, that is, "my route to school". If we examine some actual or stylized examples taken from such maps then early problems in mapping become apparent. Figure 1 shows a section of a map where not only are data drawn as pictograms but also are drawn from the child's point of view. Impermanent objects will often be placed in maps. Thus on Figure 1 we find that a car is drawn, and on many maps children may draw a dog, or their friends, or even objects which do not exist at all; simply because they want to fill in the space. If slopes are attempted, as in Figure 2, then in early mapping children will draw objects at right angles to the slope. Some children will go to great lengths not only to show curves in the road, but also to show undulations in the landscape. Thus a straight road may be drawn in serpentlike manner in order to indicate the rise and fall of the ground.

As has been mentioned, it is not until approximately the age of eight that a child is able to draw what may be called "a pilot's eye view". This phrase seems more appropriate today than using the phrase "a bird's eye view". The latter phrase may lead to such questions as "how high is the bird flying?" Young children have difficulty in drawing "from above" in what appears to be the simplest situation. If they are allowed to stand on a chair in the classroom and look down on an object it is very often impossible for them to draw that object from above even if it remains in their sight. A simple example of this is to ask a child to look at a bottle from above, and then to draw it. In

Figure 2

Figure 3

almost all cases the bottle is still drawn "from the side". Figure 3 however shows a "pilot's eye view" of a park drawn by a boy of eight. In this case he has been consistent in drawing everything from above. The trees are drawn from above, a small building with a chimney is drawn from above as are two boys and a dog. It is unfair even for adults to apply this aspect of mapping too literally, for as children will point out, features such as lighthouses and windmills are "drawn from the side" on topographical maps.

If we move from the actual drawing of objects to the problem of organizing those objects in space, we see how the difficulties are compounded. Figure 4 shows a map of "my route to school" drawn by a seven year old Chilean boy. His map appears to show that he has had to go a very long way to get to a shcool which seems to be almost next to his home. However, what he has in fact done is to plot his movements in space, that is, one right hand turn, followed by two left turns, followed by a curve in the road to reach the school. This is a very common "error" when young children are asked to draw maps. They map their movements without relation to scale. Though it could be said that some are influenced by the shape of the paper and tend to draw around the outside it is equally true that other children very soon fill the whole paper before they are half way through their journey! This however, is not an uncommon feature in adults when *they* draw maps to show people how to get from A to B.

Again it is not usually until the age of eight or nine that a child will be able to organize a map so that the relative distances are correct. The appearance of a route which has been marked in to help the viewer is a significant step forward. At this stage the child is not only able to organize space for himself, but feels confident enought to mark in a route to help the map reader. In the case of Figure 5 a number of helpful hints are given to the person for whom the map is being drawn. "My home is green and white", is supplemented by

Figure 4

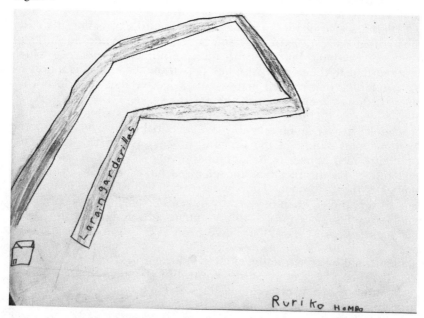

Figure 5

names of roads and telegraph poles, and in this example all the houses are drawn from the same viewpoint.

Perhaps one of the most significant features of children's early maps is that data are extremely selective. Such maps do not attempt to show everything, but rather to indicate points of reference which are important to the person who has drawn the map. This is a precursor to the idea that printed maps show selective data and do not attempt to show every feature of the earth's surface. The previous figures emphasize that if drawings or maps on a topic such as "my route to school" are seen in relation to sequential age levels, then the developmental nature of the learning process is thrown into focus. Such maps may appear to be a comparatively simple exercise but we must reflect on the fact that the children have been asked to do a number of things at once. They have been asked to observe, to recall their observations, to plot data by inventing teachniques, and ultimately they have been asked to give points of reference with reasonable accuracy. Above all, they have been asked to organize data "in space", and this is no mean task. This exercise can of course, be supplemented by constructing models of local areas, and in such activities there may be a more active control of the environment than in the abstract exercise of recalling data and plotting it on paper in a representational manner. Blaut and Stea have examined this approach in their article on mapping exercises by children as young as three years of age.[2]

The previous examples have been used merely to stress the developmental nature of early mapping skills. That is, "correct" mapping cannot be taught in a series of isolated steps. Skills, by definition, need practice, and through practice a concrete awareness grows. The question of doing exercises more than once cannot be over-emphasized. "My route to school" is not an exercise confined to kindergarten or first grade, it could be practised at any grade during school life. Techniques and skills should be seen to improve, and spatial organization should become more accurate. However, the question may well be asked as to which are the basic exercises which need to be repeated and extended? Are there exercises which could lead to a firmer acquisition of mapping skills, and ultimately to a more critical appreciation of map interpretation?

DRAWING OBJECTS FROM ABOVE

To put it as simply as possible, if we are to understand mapping, we must not only use maps frequently but we must learn how to make maps, and continue to practice making them. The following exercises are not designed to be given in chronological order, and in fact may appear random. The purpose of such exercises, however, is to involve children in practising those very basic elements in mapping

---

[2]   J. M. BLAUT & D. STEA, "Mapping at the Age of Three", *The Journal of Geography* 73, 7 (October, 1974).

whichwill be practiced and extended in later years. It is also important to re-emphasize that even these basic exercises depend on having acquired, in some measure, a knowledge of vertical and horizontal, left and right, and some understanding of the concept of "the pilot's eye view".

In her book *Fundamentals of School Geography* Olive Garnett stated that children needed to know that maps "show the space things take up on the ground."[3] Therefore some of the earliest exercises we can do with children in school is to see just how much space things take up on the ground. Drawing round objects is one of the first useful exercises. To draw round a book, a pencil box, or a lunch box, shows how much space objects take up on the ground, and also removes one of the dimensions, height. Thus a tall glass appears to take up a small space on the ground, but a chalkboard will inevitably take up a large part of a wall. This exercise is also useful in helping children to understand and to codify shapes.

A first exercise in drawing things from above can consist of asking the children to place a number of objects on their own desks, and then requesting that each child map the objects on his neighbour's desk. Or, if a classroom has desks where lids may be opened, then the objects inside could be mapped from above.

THE "ME" DIAGRAM

In an early attempt at teaching how to organize objects in space, a well-known teaching strategy, which is called a "ME" diagram may be used. Figure 6 shows such a diagram (The names of various objects have been added to the original.) This diagram is placed on the child's desk and in this way every child is automatically placed in the "correct" position in space, that is, each child's diagram is located at the point where the child happens to be sitting, and this location is the central point of reference for the map. In this exercise children are simply asked to plot one or two or more features around them. Where the diagram states "ME" the child can draw a square for his own desk. He can choose to draw the desk of a friend or friends, the teacher's desk, the book corner, where the class pet lives, the door, etc. In this way objects are both oriented and, with practice, distributed proportionately. If a child wishes to draw something behind his or her own desk, then it is very often useful to allow him to leave the desk and move round to the front while cautioning him to keep the arrow pointing in the original direction or to a fixed point in the classroom. The "ME" diagram is not as simple as it looks. To plot the first object or place is relatively easy, but even young children realize that plotting subsequent objects depends on a co-ordination of space. The diagram is also useful in developing an awareness of the body axes, "behind", "in front", "right", and "left".

---

[3] O. GARNETT, *Fundamentals in School Geography* (Harrap, 1960).

Figure 6

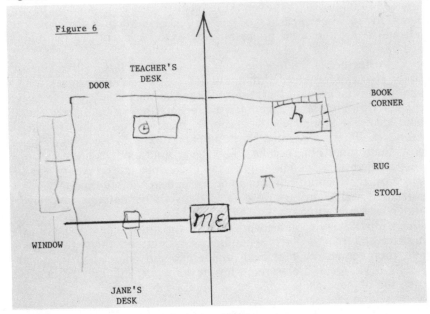

SHADOWS

Outside the classroom, two of the earliest exercises which relate to both mapping and other geographical concepts, are to be found in the drawing of shadows. One of the simplest methods is to allow the children to work in pairs and draw around each other's shadows. (In this exercise it is usually incumbent upon the teacher to state in advance that the children will clean the chalk from the playground, before the janitor complains!) Children can then have their partner draw an outline of his own body on a large sheet of paper and match it against the shadow. An extension of this is for the children to stand in the same spot later in the day and see that the shadow is now a different length. This is a first step in finding north, but at the same time shadows have a magical quality which give many children both an opportunity for creative thinking as well as aesthetic pleasure. It is also useful in identifying the reality of daylight saving.

However, it is not enough to simply say at noon "Look, your shadow is pointing to the north". Children will very quickly point out that *all* their shadows are pointing in the same direction, and in fact the shadows will be parallel one with the other. In this case "north" appears to be an arc rather than a fixed point of direction. The purpose of such simple shadow exercises related to mapping are merely starting points. They indicate certain observable features, and this perceptual input is the first step in the acquisition of a true concept of "north".

An extension of this shadow exercise is to make a shadow record on the lines of the traditional sun dial. All that is required is a
sheet of paper affixed to a drawing board with a short nail in the
centre. It is remarkable to note how long the shadows which are
cast by even a three inch nail are. Care needs to be taken in this exercise to ensure that the shadow record will remain in sunlight all
day, for it has often been the case that the shadow of a building
will cover the shadow graph as the hours pass by. The aims of these
two exercises are merely to indicate that shadow lengths change,
they become shorter or longer. It may be apparent that the sun appears at a different angle at different times of the day. However, the
use of the noon-time shadow is a first step in finding north, and the
movement of shadows, seen visibly on a playground is a most useful
precursor in carrying out similar experiments with a globe. A very
common classroom experiment is to illuminate a globe with the light
from a slide projector and to affix map pins to the globe by small
amounts of plasticine. When the globe is then spun eastwards the
shadow of the map pin will first shorten and then lengthen. This
exercise means much more to children if they have noticed their
own shadows lenghtening and shortening or have seen this happen
on a shadow record.

An interesting example of children's logic may be quoted here.
A group of second grade children were keeping a shadow record for a
whole day and at noon the teacher asked the group whether or not
they thought the shadows would now get longer or shorter. A number
of children replied that the shadows would get shorter and one of
them gave the reason as being that as the sun sank lower in the sky
the light would get weaker, the shadow would therefore get shorter,
until it "went out".

A further extension of this exercise is to take shadow readings
at the same time of day but a different times of year to see how much
longer shadows are in winter than they are in the summer at, say, ten
o'clock in the morning. This is one of the first steps in understanding
climate, and particularly the seasons. If each shadow were said to
represent a sunbeam, then each sunbeam would then have to do much
more work to heat a larger area of ground in winter than it would in
the summer. However, it has been pointed out by many geographers
that such experiments, however useful, are also paradoxical. Unless
one is careful to use the phrase that the sun "appears to move" the
experiments merely confirm that the sun moves and the earth stands
still. Fortunately the globe and map pin shadow exercise plus the
constant activity by cosmonauts in space have made this point less
difficult to understand.

Once a child has had some experience with a "ME" diagram
and in drawing round objects then such exercises can be extended. To
walk around a not too complex building and then to ask children to
draw the shape of the building is a useful starting point. This also
illustrates an aspect of relative size which puzzles many children

when they use large scale maps of buildings or are working on air photographs. Children who live in high rise blocks will complain that their block is not shown. At the same time they can easily identify a large single storey Supermarket next door to their own apartment block. The Supermarket takes up "a lot of space on the ground"; the high rise takes up little space. One could also reflect on differences in perception which must exist in children who are brought up in high rise apartments.

Children may then extend their mapping outside the school grounds. To map a street, plotting traffic signs and five hydrants is a useful exercise. At this stage children may still draw objects pictographically and at right angles to the road, but as this is a natural stage of development this factor is relatively unimportant. What is important is that they can map things accurately and have some sense of organizing objects in space. Thus if there are ten houses on a block there should be squares or drawings to illustrate those ten houses. The child could draw in detail one house which he or she finds to be interesting or attractive. An early "recall" exercise to assist children in drawing a groupe of objects from above is to ask them to draw a map of their own room or a room at home. Here one is drawing on a fundamental pool of knowledge and even first attempts at maps of this type can often be extremely successful. Children will, of course, very often only draw one view of the room, and that view will most probably be the view towards the television set. Nevertheless, such exercises allow children to utilize frames of reference which they know well, and also to explain them to an observer. The "ME" diagram can now be extended to the local world. Instead of having "ME" in the centre the school could be placed in the centre. The child can then plot a number of buildings in the immedaite environment and try and organize those in space (Figure 7). As indicated by Bentley in his book on children's mapping such exercises help children to extend into the unknown from a firm foundation of what *is* known.[4]

AERIAL PHOTOGRAPHS

All maps show discrete material. For example, a topographical map of a city will "show" the streets and the extent of the urban area. Hills and valleys may be there, illustrated by contours, but they are not a dominant feature of the map. In other words, the hills and valleys do not show up very well while the urban area does. In this case it is always useful to introduce aerial photographs as soon as possible to complement any local maps which are being used.

There are two types of aerial photographs, oblique and vertical. The low oblique type of photograph is often the most useful to children, since it represents a fairly normal point of view, as from a hill or as in the view when landing at an airport. However, there are prob-

---

4   J. C. BENTLEY *et al.*, *The Use of Maps in School* (Blackwells, 1975).

Figure 7

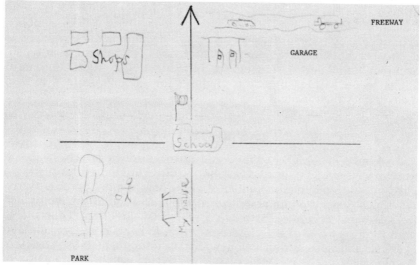

lems in oblique photographs in that features in the foreground may mask other features, and there is also a problem of a variable scale which alters with distance. Vertical photographs give a truer view of the distribution of data on the surface of the earth and correspond more or less exactly to a map, particularly with regard to the phrase "maps show the space things take up on the ground". There will inevitably be problems in identifying relief features since the nature of the photograph tends to flatten height (though this may be overcome by the use of stereoscopes). Nevertheless the vertical air photograph is extremely useful in helping children identify their own local area and acquiring some concept of the distribution of buildings and relative distances in an area which is known to them. Stea and Blaut point to the fact that in their experiments with children in kindergarten such children can make identification from aerial photographs without recourse to formal schooling, and that flying was not common in the groups tested.[5]

It is just as important to orient an air photograph as it is to orient a map. Therefore, if an air photograph is being studied in the classroom, it should be turned round the "right way". In this case all the objects on the photograph and the children themselves are correctly co-ordinated in space.

It should now be possible to build on such early mapping exercises as "my route to school". This map could be drawn again with an emphasis on greater accuracy and direct questions asked such as "could your friend use this map to find his way from school to your

---

    [5]   D. STEA and James M. BLAUT, "Some Preliminary Observations on Spatial Learning in School Children", in R. M. DOWNS & D. STEA (eds.), *Image of Environment* (Aldine Publishing Co., 1973).

house ?'' Verbal exercises also have their place in these early stages of mapping. The exercise ''Can you give good directions'' is a useful way of thinking out loud. Since most concepts have verbal symbols, and since it is normal within conceptual development to attempt to define concepts, then the giving of directions is an exercise in recall, accuracy, and verbal fluency. It is interesting to note that most adults prefer written directions to move for example from A to B in a city rather than using a map.

''CLASSROOM'' MAPS

A map of the classroom could now be drawn in greater detail. This is a very common exercise but is often attempted too early. A child needs to practice a number of skills before more precise exercises which depend on an ability to manipulate a larger number of objects grouped according to relative scale and direction. To ask children to draw maps of the classroom *to scale* is an extremely difficult exercise and adds a dimension which is difficult at most stages of development in the elementary school. Scale, which is a function of ratio, will be discussed later.

MAP SYMBOLS

We now come to the introduction of the map symbols. In many cases children will make up their own map symbols as they draw their own maps. These will normally be pictograms and the idea of grouping these pictograms into a key or legend is one which usually has to be made by the teacher. Children rarely collect and codify such symbols on their own. However, it is an important rule of thumb that map symbols should only be introduced when and where necessary. It is not necessary to learn, copy, and practice all the map symbols used on topographical maps at one sitting. One useful way of introducing map symbols is to use the ''Treasure Island'' approach.

For this, a teacher or a child can make up a story which has at the end the burial of a pirate treasure. Here is a short story on this theme written by an eleven year old boy.

> The pirate captain ordered the boat lowered and went ashore with two of his men. They disappeared among the trees and the crew went swimming or drank lemonade. Suddenly they heard the sound of shots in the distance and a great flock of parrots flew out of the trees and up into the air. Nothing more was heard all day and the crew began to be worried. As the sun began to set the pirate captain came out of the trees and staggered down towards the shore. They went and collected him and found that he was wounded. He told the other pirates that the two men he had taken with him had jumped him and run away with the treasure. He had tried to stop them but they had fired at him and wounded him. All this was a lie. He had let the two pirates dig a hole and put the treasure in and then he had shot them and buried them with the treasure. He had wounded himself with his knife and torn his own clothes to pretend that they had done it. The pirate captain went back into his cabin and sat down to

draw a map so that he would be able to find the treasure when he came
back another day. The crew were mad that they had lost the treasure and
sailed out of the bay to try and find the other pirates but they never did.

Two maps may be drawn from this exercise: first, a map could be
drawn of the Treasure Island on an individual basis. Certain features
need to be mapped in order to find the treasure, e.g. a route to the
treasure though details could be left to individual imagination. Map
symbols of an unconventional nature way very well appear at this
point. A second map on a larger scale may well have to be drawn in
the vicinity of the treasure to allow the treasure hunter to reach the
precise spot.

An extension of this Treasure Island exercise is to divide a class
into groups and allow each group to bury some type of "treasure".
Each group could then draw a map to lead another group to the buried
treasure. This is an exercise where accuracy is re-inforced by peer
pressure from other groups. If group A draws an accurate map so that
group B can find the treasure buried by A, then group A will be un-
derstandably annoyed if group B's map is inaccurate and prevents the
treasure being found. This is also a useful time to twin the idea of
treasure maps with preliminary exercises on scale lines.

SCALE

The use of a scale on maps is a complex conceptual step for
children. Between the ages of ten and eleven seems an appropriate
time to approach scale as a mathematical exercise, however, before
this certain practical exercises could be initiated.

The aims of such exercises should be to allow the child to move
towards the acquisition of a concept of scale, that is, what scale really
means. A definition such as "we shortened everything so that we can
get it down on the paper" is an indication that a child has some
knowledge of scale. The phrase such as "we measure things" indicates that scale may simply be equated with some form of measurement. The understanding of both scale and area needs mental preparation.

In the mid nineteen sixties a large number of school children
were tested in Bristol, England to see whether or not they had acquired a concept of area. Almost all the children could explain that area
meant "length times breadth" but over 40% in subsequent testing had
no concept of what area really *was*. Thus exercises are needed to
prepare children, in a practical way, to tackle this problem so that
ultimately they will acquire the concept of scale.

Practical measurement is essential, and the use of the non-
formal unit should precede the use of the formal unit. A useful approach is to ask children to estimate distances by means of arm-
spans, wool pieces, or the use of a metre trundle wheel (sometimes
known as a "click wheel"). A table of such estimates follows, and it

should be noted that a child's definition of "estimate" is "a careful guess".

What we measured	"We thought it was"	"It really was"
The corridor	80 clicks	33 clicks
Across the playground	150 clicks	142 clicks

(The children then changed to counting metres instead of "clicks".)

From the flag to the road	25 metres	30 metres
Along the front of the school	60 metres	55 metres
Mr. Harvey's garden	50 metres	50 metres

As Figure 8 indicates, various distances can be measured and plotted in a simple manner, and scale lines can be drawn. After practice, it can be pointed out that a constant scale is of more use than an odd scale such as 37 clicks. The scale line can be reduced to a more conventional unit of measurement, 5 clicks or 10 clicks, etc.

It does not follow that the children will immediately see scale in terms of formal measurement. A query asked of a child in British Columbia, "How far is it from Powell River to Vancouver?" elicited the answer "Two ferries". This was a reasonable expression of time and distance, and also a highly individual approach to scale.

It is but a short step from using the informal unit to replacing it with a formal unit. In this case actual measurements can be plotted and mapped, for example, from the climbing frame to the monkey bars, from the climbing frame to the classroom door etc. The actual distance in metres can be mapped, and a conventional scale line drawn at the foot of the map.

A further way of introducing scale is to use a sheet of squared paper where each square could represent one click on the trundle wheel or one metre, depending on whether the child was using a for-

Figure 8

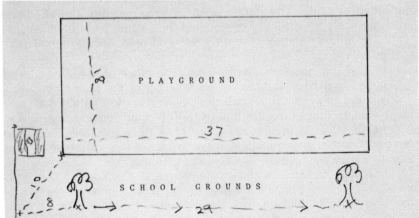

mal or informal unit. As Figure 9 indicates this method is also useful for drawing the shape of the building. Figure 9 shows the front of a school building, the children went along the outside of it with a trundle wheel and every time it clicked they marked one side of one square. If they were required to turn a corner they "turned a corner" on paper. In this way they were easily able to map part of the front of a building, and a number of sheets of squared paper joined together produced, eventually, a ground plan of the whole building. In this case the use of a one-metre scale occurred almost incidentally. The extension of this activity is to apply the scale exercises to the "treasure hunts" mentioned in previous paragraphs. In the latter exercise accuracy becomes extremely important to the children concerned.

APPROACHING TOPOGRAPHICAL MAPS

It is said that a child is more likely to become a reader if he sees his parents read at home. Similarly, children will assimilate ideas about maps if they are surrounded by them. A map from a gas station is better than no map at all, and a cluster of map pins on a classroom map which shows where each child lives is an exercise which can be done as early as first grade. Globes, maps of the world, and maps of Canada can be displayed at any grade level. Children will benefit by their being in evidence although it is doubtful whether or not young children will be able to understand the significance of the distribution of land and sea on a world map. World maps are further complicated by the problem of map projections.

It is for this reason that active work on maps remains so important. The different parts of the world new Canadians have come from can be used as primary points of location. Similarly acquiring some

Figure 9

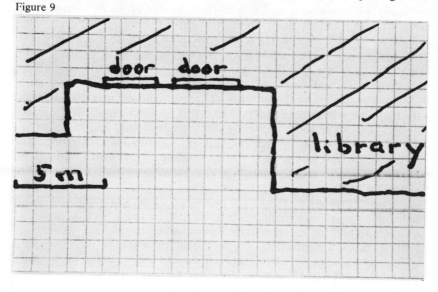

idea of general distances (for example, "How long would it take to fly to India, how long would it take to fly to Australia?"), are all exercises which ultimately lead to a mental map of the world, though such mental maps are very often incomplete in adults.

The use of local topographical maps still remains the best introduction to formal mapping. For a child even to see the name of his town at the foot of the map, or to identify the river which is known and has been seen, or an island or a place where friends or relatives live, all are a helpful introduction to mapping. Such data needs no precise teaching, but may lead to questioning about maps and what they show.

One of the problems of mapping is that most topographical maps are out of date and the date of publication or revision should be pointed out to children. Children are quick to spot that maps lack contemporary details. A new bridge may have been built, an urban area may have been extended and this may not be shown on the local map which is on the classroom wall. Similarly, because they are so often out of date, maps may well have on them features which have subsequently disappeared. Children may be puzzled to find an area marked as "swamp" or "marsh" on a map which they currently know as a park by the side of the river.

Some indication of the size of an area can be achieved by making up a map mosaic. For this, adjoining local large scale map sheets can be placed on the classroom floor. The borders of the maps can be folded inwards, and the maps laid side by side to form a mosaic. When this is done the maps should be oriented as the mosaic is being made. It is perhaps not sufficiently taken into consideration that for younger children maps mean much more if they can be viewed from *above* with the map lying horizontally. It is normal to display things vertically on classroom walls, but the transfer of co-ordinates from horizontal to vertical poses real problems for many children. The ability to stand *above* a correctly oriented map, to point and say "the sea is over there" and to know that the sea *is* in that direction is a significant aspect in the organization of space.

Topographical maps will, however, mean more to children if they have made maps themselves. There is a "language" concerned with mapping which needs to be learned in an active and participatory manner. This experience is best gained when young and before children have had "subjects" locked into rigid compartments. An active approach can lead to a greater understanding of the world and can be a starting point for many other types of activities which are related to the environment.

Children require frames of reference at an early age. If these cognitive patterns are firmly established then the possible range of applications will be greater. It is not possible to take the genesis of mapping skills for granted. A great deal of work in modern child psychology has shown that children do not only reason differently from adults, but that they have different views of the world.

Similarly, it has been stressed in this chapter that children need to practice and extend the activities described. This can sometimes present a problem when children say that they "did that last year" or that they "know" it. There is a natural sense of grievance in asking people to reconsider facts they claim to "know". However, as Bloom has suggested[6] learning experiences need to be increasingly sophisticated though they may continue to start from the same base.

Maps have been referred to as "a representation of space". Their three principal features, direction, a key or legend, and a scale are features which are not presented clinically in the early years in school. Nevertheless children can assimilate data to provide them with a structured background of knowledge which can be called on as tasks become more complex.

---

[6] B. S. BLOOM, *Taxonomy of Educational Objectives* (Longmans, 1965).

ENVIRONMENTAL PERCEPTION

K. G. DUECK
Department of Education
University of Calgary

In the nineteenth century geographers were concerned with the problem of explaining environmental behavior or man-land relationships and chose to explain man in terms of land. However, the theory of environmentalism collapsed and geographers were forced to seek elsewhere for explanations.

Three concepts evolved to express clearly and simply the interaction of man and his environment. The first of these was the concept of landscape which entails the analysis of human interaction with the physical world through the study of man's impact upon the land. The second was the concept of ecosystem, which attempted to explore direct interactions between man and land in relatively simple circumstances. The third and perhaps most complex of these concepts was environmental perception—an effort to evaluate man-environmental relationships by means of the decisions and value systems used by man to interpret and influence his world.[1]

This paper includes a review of and a guide to the literature on the concept of environmental perception. The review is divided into three sections. First, an attempt is made to develop some conceptual distinctions as a theory base. The second section focuses on the empirical research and theory about the development of cognition of the larger physical environment. The final section examines literature from the educational and curricular orientation related to environmental perception.

I.—DEFINITIONS AND CONCEPTUAL DISTINCTIONS

The literature related to the concept of environmental perception contains a number of terms which need clarification. First, it is necessary to clarify the terms spatial cognition and cognitive representation which encompass the more specific terms of cognitive mapping or mental maps used both in environmental behavior literature (e.g., Downs, 1970)[2] and cultural geography (e.g., Gould, 1966).[3]

---

[1] P. ENGLISH, Landscape, ecosystem and environmental perception: concepts in cultural geography", *The Journal of Geography*, April 1968.

[2] R. M. DOWNS, "The cognitive structure of an urban shopping centre", *Environment and Behavior*, June 1970, 13-39.

[3] P. R. GOULD, "On mental maps", in P. W. ENGLISH, R. G. MAYFIELD (Eds.), *Man, Space and Environment*, (New York: Oxford University Press, 1972).

Each theorist who discusses representation refers to an external representation such as a drawing or map.

Internal representations can only be inferred from external representations (maps, verbal reports, drawings) or overt behavior. The external representations are of interest to the degree that they shed some light upon the development of the internal representations of the enviroment. Clearly, a crucial assumption in all this research and theory is that the internal operation powers are in congruence with the external representations.

In the literature the terms cognitive maps and cognitive mapping are commonly used. The environment need not necessarily be represented in cartographic form; the map is only one form of intellectual representation of the environment; others being a painting, a prose selection, a musical score or lines of peotry.

A further distinction must be drawn between cognition and perception. Cognition embraces all modes of knowing including perceiving, thinking, imagining, reasoning and remembering. Thus, the idea of spatial cognition would seem to include perception. A closely allied view is held by Wapner and Werner,[4] who treat perception as a subsystem of cognition. Knowledge about the environment is constructed in many ways, including perceptual inputs. In turn, perceptual preferences are influenced by the cognitive structures developed by the individual. Perception and spatial cognition are two separate but reciprocating processes.

The concept of perception was developed in the field of psychology, and other disciplines have both modified it and widened its applicability. Various theorists and researchers have made explicit statements concerning the process of perception. Perception, according to Bruner,[5] can be considered a process of categorization in which the organism moves inferentially from cues to the categorical identity. Another psychologist suggests that perception is the experience of objects and events which are here and ensue from sensory processes as distinguished from memory.[6]

A number of typologies have been constructed, contrasting persons whose typical ways of experiencing the world differ in some way. These typologies include contrasting modes such as analyzer and synthesizer, being subjective and objective, or field-dependent and field-independent.

It has also been suggested that various variables—set, affect, inputs, personality, experience—influence perception of the environment. Set was found to be facilitating when appropriate to the situa-

        4   H. WERNER & S. WAPNER, "Toward a general theory of perception", *Psychological Review*. 47 (1952), 324-338.

        5   J.S. BRUNER, "On perceptual readiness", *Psychological Review*, 67 (1970), 123-152.

        6   O. MAGNE, *Perception and Learning* (Uppsula: Appelsbergs Boktryckeri, 1952).

tion but misleading and an impediment to perception when unsuitable to the situation.

Gardner Murphy, after a series of studies, asserted that affect is a strong factor in perceptual learning—"Through all this, I believe, runs a central theme : the perceptual field comes to take on a structure in which the acceptable, the good, the satisfying tends to take the dominant position."[7] Werner and Wapner affirm Murphy's position by pointing out that the perceptual properties of an object or the environment depend on the way in which stimuli from the object or environment affect the organism and on the manner in which the organism reacts to the stimuli. In contrast, Fishbein[8] argues that knowledge of an individual's affect toward some object or the environment does not ensue with an accurate prediction of that individual's behavior. He suggests that the conceptualization of an attitude and its hypothetical links with behavior are faulty. He replaces a holistic concept of an attitude with a formulation containing three components : cognitions or beliefs, affect or attitudes and conations or behavioral intentions. The belief component of Fishbein's model is relevant to the concept of cognitive map. The three components may not always be correlated which results in weakened links between attitude and behavior. Fishbein hastens to point out that attitudes, beliefs and behavioral intentions, although often disjointed, are frequently brought into line with actual behavior.

Other researchers proffer the hypothesis that perception varies from person to person in accord with selective forces provided by culturally determined experiences. "At this point," state Segall, Campbell and Herskovits,[9] "there is little unequivocal evidence of cultural influences on perception." Thus, if cultural differences are to be found, they are likely to be the results of culturally mediated differences in experience rather than manifestations of biological differences among cultural groups.

The role of personality factors in the process of environmental perception has been discussed by a number of investogators. The small number of empirical studies which have employed the concept of personnality as an explanatory construct include the studies of fluoridation controversies, hazard perception and attitudes toward environmental conditions such as snow, wind, rain. The personality differences seem endless, yet we can begin to distinguish those individuals who are innovators and those who are not; those who are sensitive to their environment and those who are not; those who prefer an urban environment and those who wish a rural environment.

---

[7] G. MURPHY, "Affect and perceptual learning", *Psychological Review*, 63 (1956), 1-15

[8] M. FISHBEIN, "Attitudes and the prediction of behavior", in M. FISHBEIN, (Ed.), *Readings in Attitude Theory and Measurement*, (New York : Wiley, 1967b), 447-492.

[9] M. SEGALL, D. CAMPBELL, & M. HERSKOVITS, *The Influence of Culture on Visual Perception* (New York : The Bobbs-Merrill Company, Inc.), 262-287.

The work of Held and associates[10] suggests that motor experience and sensorimotor interaction with the environment are important to the development of perception. Their experiments indicate that individuals exposed to equivalent sensory stimulation—e.g., visual—but differential opportunities to interact with an experienced environment, show different degrees of perceptual attainment. Specifically, the less motor-environment interaction available to an individual, the less precise the perception of his environment becomes.

II.—DEVELOPMENT OF SPATIAL COGNITION OF THE LARGER PHYSICAL ENVIRONMENT

Attention will now be directed to the development of spatial cognition of large scale environments. Much of the research in this area has been conducted by cultural geographers, under the heading of environmental perception.

The concept of environmental perception assumes that each man has an "image" of the world and that within a given culture these images are largely shared. Not only does perception depend upon the stimulus present and the capabilities of the sense organs, but it also varies with the individual's past history and present set or attitude acting through values, wants, memories and expectations. The present stage of research in environmental perception is such that no real body of theory has been developed. Another factor common to research in this branch of geography is its recency of development. A result of its recent development is the lack of a well-defined methodology.

The search for effective methods of measuring perception of the environment and attempts to develop a methodology help explain another characteristic of this geographic concept—namely, its interdisciplinary nature. Much of the work represents a fusion of ideas from many fields. It places geographers in close association with other social scientists (e.g., psychologists, sociologists, anthropologists) whose queries are somewhat similar.

The literature in geography related to environmental perception is quite varied. A statement which outlines the complexity and breadth of geographic concern with man's perception of his environment has been given by Lowenthal,[11] who states that the concern lies with "the relation between the world outside and the pictures in our heads."

In dealing with perception, it is recognized that psychological studies have been conducted largely within the laboratory and have

---

[10]   R. HELD, & J. REKOSH, "Motor-sensory feedback and the geometry of visual space", *Science* 141 (1963), 722-723.

[11]   D. LOWENTHAL, "Geography, experience and imagination: towards a geographical epistomology", *Annals of the Association of American Geographers*, 51 (1961), 241-261.

dealt with very limited physical phenomena. There is doubt as to their applicability to observations of more complex and gross phenomena (Hewitt (1969)[12] investigated the theoretical ground for expressing extreme events in probabilistic terms. At this point the interest of geographers in perception converged with those of psychologists, sociologists, city planners and architects who also were trying to specify perception and its implications (Burton and Kates, 1964).[13] Out of the concern for perception of floods come the first AAG symposium on problems of perception, a series of investigations dealing with perception of differing facets of the environment such as drought, recreational water, reservoirs, water supply alternatives, water recycling and Saarinen's geographic review of perception literature (Saarinen, 1969).[14]

Geographers are no longer studying the perception of the environment in broad general ways or as an incidental part of a larger study. Instead, the focus has been directed to the investigation of people in an attempt to determine their perception of the environment at varying scales, beginning with the individual and neighborhood to progressively larger portions of the environment to include a world view.

Several studies concentrate on those spheres of the environment that impinge directly on the individual. Julian Wolpert,[15] for example, employed the term "action space" in speaking about the immediately perceived environment and "decision environment" to cover the larger space in which decision-makers attempt to cope with the problem of the environment. In discussing this problem, Sonnenfeld[16] divides the environment into four distinct sections of progressively more limited scope; the geographical environment, the operational environment, the perceptual environment and the behavioral environment.

Other human geographers have concerned themselves primarily with environmental preferences and decisions. In the paper "On Mental Maps," Gould discusses the theoretical implications of environmental preferences which can be made for spatial behavior. Similarly, other researchers have analyzed the components in a physical

---

[12] K. HEWITT, "Probabilistic approaches to discrete natural events: a review and theoretical discussion", *Natural Hazard Working Paper No. 8*, Department of Geography, The University of Toronto, 1969.

[13] I. BURTON & R. W. KATES, "Perception of natural hazards in resources management", *Natural Resources Journal*, 3, (1964), 412-441.

[14] T. SAARINEN, *Perception of Environment* (Washington, D.C.: Association of American Geographers, Commission on College Geography, Resource Paper No. 5, 1969).

[15] J. WOLPERT, "Behavioral aspects of decision to migrate", *Papers of Regional Science Association*, 15 (1965), 159-169.

[16] J. SONNENFELD, "Geography, perception and the behavioral environment", in P. W. ENGLISH & R. G. MAYFIELD (Eds.), *Man, Space and Environment*, (New York: Oxford University Press), 1972, 244-251.

environment with detailed examination of human attitudes and responses to different environments and stimuli.

The most detailed and exact research in the study of man's perception lies in the interdisciplinary area of knowledge about personal space. The work of Hall[17] is a basic approach to the study of "proxemics" or personal space. This subject is further explored by Sommers[18] who identifies some of the invisible boundaries which protect and compartmentalize each individual. The partterning of behavioral responses when invasion, crowding or spatial restructuring occurs was explored in laboratory-like settings such as libraries and hospital wards.

The field of environmental perception has incorporated the concept of "imageability" with its borrowed methodology from psychology and sociology, numerous but ill-defined concepts, and incomplete theory. The concept of "image" was introduced by C. C. Trowbridge[19] in 1913 when he identified "ego-centric" and "domi-centric" as terms denoting the two modes of environmental observation he noted. However, not until the late 1950s with the appearance of Kenneth Boulding's *The Image*[20] was interest revived in the construct of imagery and environmental perception.

Prominent among the antecedents of present research is the seminal research of Lynch (1960),[21] which introduced concepts and techniques for eliciting, organizing, and analyzing the elements of city images held by adults in three urban areas (Boston, Jersey City and Los Angeles). Subsequent studies of urban images, using modifications of Lynch's approach, include the work of Lee (1963-64),[22] Carr and Schissler (1969),[23] Appleyard (1970),[24] and Lowrey (1970).[25] Each study contributes to a beginning theory of imageability.

Simultaneously, a field of study by geographers and psychologists has focused upon the cognitive mappings of the urban environ-

[17]   E. T. HALL, *The Silent Language* (New York: Doubleday, 1959); Id., *The Hidden Dimension* (New York: Doubleday, 1966).

[18]   R. SOMMERS, *Personal Space: The Behavioral Basic of Design* (New York: Prentice-Hall, 1969).

[19]   C. C. TROWBRIDGE, "Fundamental methods of orientation and imaginary maps", *Science*, 38 (1913), 888-897.

[20]   K. E. BOULDING, *The Image* (Ann Arbor: University of Michigan Press, 1956).

[21]   K. LYNCH, *The Image of a City* (Cambridge, Mass.: MIT Press, 1960).

[22]   T. LEE, "Urban neighborhood as a socio-spatial scheme", *Human Relations*, 21 (1963), 241-267.

[23]   S. CARR and D. SCHISSLER, "The City as a Trip", *Environment and Behavior*, June, 1969, 7-36.

[24]   D. APPLEYARD, "Styles and methods of structuring a city", *Environment and Behavior*, June 1970, 100-117.

[25]   R. A. LOWREY, "Distance concepts of urban residents", *Environment and Behavior*, June 1970, 52-75.

ment by children and adolescents (e.g., Blaut, et al, 1970;[26] Ladd, 1970;[27] Maurer, 1970;[28] Fine, 1967;[29] Tindal, 1971;[30] Andrew, 1973;[31] Dueck, 1976[32] and 1978).[33] This group of researchers has also attempted to probe the differences in images held by children of different ethnic groups. Several researchers have concluded that a major determinant of the form and content of the image or content of cognitive maps is the spatial range of activity in which individuals move. For all groups, with duly noted exceptions, the cognitive mapping gradually increased in range and accuracy thus indicating a developmental process in the perception of the environment.

III.—ENVIRONMENTAL PERCEPTION AND ITS PLACE IN EDUCATION AND CURRICULUM

Pertinent to this paper is a consideration of the concept of environmental perception for education and specifically for curriculum at the school level. One curriculum component which is directly related to this concern is geography and its relationship to the other social sciences.

A perusal of the literature of educators and curriculum specialists indicates that subject matter broadly defined as geography has been taught for many years. Historically speaking, the role of geography in school curriculum has been vague and undefined. Geography was considered to be the first "social" subject taught in schools, but it was often an incidental part of a curriculum which emphasized reading, writing and arithmetic. Beginning in the 1920s geography was taught through the unified approach with social studies or as a separate subject. The unified approach received more emphasis when James[34] wrote, "It is time the hard core of geography be returned to the social studies."

[26] J. M. BLAUT, G. S. McCLEARY & A. S. BLAUT, "Environmental mapping in young children", *Environment and Behavior*, December 1970, 335-349.

[27] F. C. LADD, "Black youths view their environment", *Environment and Behavior*, June 1970, 74-101.

[28] R. MAUER, "The Image of Neighbourhood and City Among Black-Anglo-and Mexican American Children", M.A. thesis, The University of Houston, 1970.

[29] P. FINE, "A Child's View of His World" in H. L. MILLER and M. SMILEY (Eds.) *Education in the Metropolis* (New York: The Free Press, 1967), 222-238.

[30] M. A. TINDAL, *Home Range of Black Elementary Children* (Chicago: Environment Research Group, 1971).

[31] H. F. ANDREWS, "Home range and urban knowledge of school-age children", *Environment and Behavior*, March 1973, 73-86.

[32] K. G. DUECK, "Imageability: implications for teaching geography", *The Journal of Geography*, March 1976, 135-148.

[33] K. G. DUECK, "Mittelwertsvergleich der Testleistungen nach Schiltypen", in Helmut SCHRETTENBRUNNER, *Der Erdkundeunterricht* (Stuttgart: Ernst Klett Verlag, 1978), 9-19.

[34] P. E. JAMES, "The hard core of geography", in *New Viewpoints of Geography*, Twenty-ninth Yearbook of the National Council of Social Studies (Washington, D.C.: National Education Association, 1954).

Many definitions of geography have been stated. Richard Hartshorne[35] defined the field when he wrote, "Stated simply, geography is the study of the earth as the home of man." Preston James stated geography was that field of learning in which characteristics of certain places on the earth's surface are examined; the arrangement of things within an area are studied and the connections and movements between areas are investigated.

McNee[36] suggests "that geography is what geographers share" : a few key values and concepts, a research method and several basic research traditions. He states that all geographers value comprehensive explanations, the use of maps as a means of recording and transmitting information and, direct observavion as a procedure for gathering information.

Although various geographers have suggested some basic generalizations of geography, Hanna[37] and associates evolved a detailed framework for selecting and structuring the geographic content and map skills. Their design has two dimensions: scope and sequence. The logic of sequence emerges from the fact that everyone lives simultaneously within a set of enlarging but interdependent communities of men. The framework begins by emphasizing the oldest, smallest and most intimate group—the family community—and gradually, systematically moves to larger communities—the school community, the neighborhood, the local community, the region and the national community. The scope of the plan focuses upon basic human activities including: transportation, communication, education, recreation, governing and so on.

Recently, changes and revival have come into being at both the elementary and secondary school levels. At the elementary level increasing emphasis is placed on involving children in learning specifically identified geographic concepts and generalizations. In many cases children are learning by using procedures similar to those a geographer might use. In addition, children are required to think at higher levels of cognition.

For most students in junior and senior high schools, geography still means an inventory type of study of the world, country by country. There are exceptions to these statements (e.g., High School Geography Project) and the exceptions are becoming more numerous. The following summary compiled by Angus Gunn[38] lists some of the salient features of new developments and contrasts them.

[35]   R. HARTSHORNE, *The Nature of Geography*, (Lancaster, P.A.: Association of American Geographers, 1939), 130-148.

[36]   R. McNEE, "An approach to understanding current structures of geography", in I. MORRISSET (Ed.), *Concepts and Structures in the New Social Science Curricula*. (New York: Hold, Rinehart and Winston, 1967). 57-60.

[37]   P.R. HANNA, *Geography in the Teaching of Social Studies: Concepts and Skills* (Boston: Houghton Mifflin, 1966).

[38]   A. GUNN, "Evaluation of geographic learning in secondary schools", in D.G. KURFMAN (Ed.), *Evaluation in Geographic Education* (Belmont, Calif.: Fearon Publishers, 1971), 41-52.

The Old Geography	*The New Geography*
(1) Concept was of child as	(1) Concept of child as active and communicating
(2) Encouragement of memorization	(2) Encouragement of inquiry
(3) Emphasis on static conditions	(3) Emphasis on dynamic conditions
(4) Preoccupation with factual detail	(4) Guiding concern with models and general principles
(5) Tendency to team history and geography	(5) Tendency to team with social sciences; physical and biological sciences

There has been emphasis upon geography as a knowledge-centered and skill-centered education. However, recent writing directs attention to another area—the fulfillment-centered curriculum. This is a geography about which limited literature eixists. It is a personal geography and rests upon the assumption that the future salvation of man lies within the individual as he seeks to develop self-reliance, self-fulfillment and self-acceptance. This personal geography formulates the following cycle of purposes for geography in education. The assumptions implicit in the cycle are that a child's growth in adequacy as a person depends upon his perception of himself; as the perception becomes more positive he is able to be more accepting of experience; that this greater openness leads to a larger repertoire of meaning and this, in turn, enhances his perception or view of himself within his environment.

Figure 1.   Model of Personal Geography*

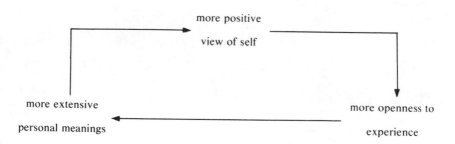

more positive

view of self

more extensive

personal meanings

more openness to

experience

However, the main thrust of this section of the paper is to come to a better understanding of the concept of environmental perception and the implications for educational practices. The concepts of spatial cognition and environmental perception are introduced in the 1970

* This figure is adapted from two diagrams in *Perceiving, Behaving, Becoming: A New Focus for Education*, 1962 Yearbook of Association for Supervision and Curriculum Development (Washington, D.C.: ASCD), 1962.

National Council of Social Studies Yearbook.[39] The discussion consists of two main sections : (1) broad scholarly studies which are concerned with the history of attitudes toward nature, and (2) current concepts of mental maps and how they are formed.

Seemingly, primary and secondary school geography and social studies classes spend a great amount of time on nonspatial aspects of geography. Spatial cognition and environmental perception continue to be neglected by educators engaged in the study of learning. Cartography as such is often not taught at all, and maps serve as an (often, as they are used, dispensible) adjunct—to other aspects of study— when they are not being used merely as coloring exercises.

---

[39]   Philip BACON, *Focus on Geography—Key Concepts and Teaching Strategies* (Washington, D.C. : National Council for the Social Studies, 40th Yearbook, 1970).

LE PROBLÈME DU VOCABULAIRE DANS L'ENSEIGNEMENT DE LA GÉOGRAPHIE

RÉAL GUAY
Université Laval

I. — INTRODUCTION : L'EXPOSÉ DU PROBLÈME

L'apprentissage et l'utilisation d'une terminologie spécialisée posent de sérieux problèmes au jeune élève qui s'initie à la géographie. Le professeur lui-même éprouve souvent des difficultés à faire le choix des termes à enseigner de préférence à d'autres, à l'intérieur du sujet traité. Pourtant, il s'agit là d'un acte primordial, puisque la terminologie utilisée véhicule les connaissances de base que l'élève devra apprendre. Il est alors facile d'imaginer qu'un choix mal fait puisse engendrer des problèmes d'apprentissage chez l'enfant et qu'on porte atteinte sérieusement à l'efficacité de l'enseignement donné pour les années à venir. Les bases sont toujours d'une importance capitale.

Par ailleurs, on pourrait croire que le professeur puisse se fier uniquement à son bon jugement et à son expérience, et qu'on n'ait aucunement besoin de statistiques pour connaître quels sont les mots les plus judicieux à enseigner dans un premier temps à ceux qui débutent en géographie. Toutefois, des enquêtes élaborées ont montré que les déficiences sont nombreuses en matière de vocabulaire géographie et que les concepts véhiculés par la terminologie sont loin d'être conformes à la vérité. Le problème est réel et sérieux.

Afin de bien cerner ce problème de la terminologie géographique, il nous faut prendre un peu de recul, car il est de ceux qui se situent dans un contexte beaucoup plus vaste qu'on pourrait le croire au premier abord. Il s'inscrit, en effet, à l'intérieur du problème général de l'acquisition du langage dont on ne peut faire fi dans le cas présent.

Instrument de communication, le langage tend au dialogue : l'acte de parole comporte à la fois un pôle émetteur et un pôle récepteur. L'enfant qui s'initie à cette technique de transmission de messages doit comprendre ce qui lui est dit, comme il doit apprendre à parler. La langue de la géographie n'échappe pas à ce principe fondamental. Et, si l'on veut que l'enseignement géographique dispensé au jeune élève soit efficace, des études approfondies s'imposent à partir des lois d'acquisition du langage commun.

C'est dans cette perspective que le présent article s'inscrit. Signalons immédiatement qu'il n'a pas la prétention de régler tous les problèmes en ce domaine. Ils sont, en effet, beaucoup trop vastes pour qu'on y arrive si rapidement. Toutefois, nous nous proposons d'apporter un certain éclairage sur la question; éclairage qui, nous l'espérons, permettra à d'autres, par la suite, d'arriver à des solutions adéquates.

II. — LES ENQUÊTES SUR L'ACQUISITION DU VOCABULAIRE GÉOGRAPHIQUE

Une fin importante de tout enseignement est l'efficacité, avons-nous dit précédemment. Si le professeur déploie tant d'efforts pour préparer et exposer son sujet, c'est qu'il vise à un apprentissage rapide et en profondeur de la part de ses élèves. L'acquisition des connaissances est donc la norme de vérification de l'efficacité d'un enseignement. Or, en géographie, d'importantes enquêtes ont prouvé que les connaissances des élèves sont loin de correspondre à tout l'effort qu'on déploie dans l'enseignement de cette discipline. Ces enquêtes sur les connaissances géographiques des élèves ont porté essentiellement sur la terminologie qui véhicule les concepts géographiques. Elles ont mis en évidence que les élèves utilisent un vocabulaire qui provient de connaissances non seulement imprécises, mais souvent erronées. L'efficacité d'un enseignement ne se vérifie pas dans la quantité, c'est-à-dire la masse des connaissances transmises, mais bien plutôt dans un choix judicieux des données de base, générales dans les débuts, et dont on doit assurer une bonne assimilation. Or, c'est la facilité à rattacher à un vocabulaire précis des connaissances, précises elles aussi, qui s'avère révélatrice d'un enseignement efficace. Et, c'est le but premier de tout enseignement.

À cause de l'importance de ces enquêtes pour étayer nos affirmations, arrêtons-nous quelque peu à les considérer afin de connaître ce qui s'en dégage.

Dès 1959, Berenice M. Casper déposait une thèse de doctorat[1] après avoir enquêté auprès de plusieurs milliers d'élèves et de professeurs des États-Unis sur l'acquisition des concepts géographiques. Prenant conscience des difficultés nombreuses et ardues que posait une transmission de qualité de ces concepts à travers la terminologie, Berenice M. Casper affirmait, dans un chapitre intitulé "Problems of Geographic Education" :

> The general vocabulary is multitudinous, extremely technical and factual to a great degree. Teachers have tendency to think that children have mastered these concepts when they can use them usily. In reality they often do not understand the symbols. Verbalism with young children

---

[1] B. M. CASPER, *Scope and Sequence of Geographic Education in the Modern School Curriculum Grades four through twelve*, thèse (PH.D.), Lincoln, University of Nebraska, 1959, 331 pages.

is especially prevalent in concepts remote from the environment of the child in time and space. It is difficult to provide the necessary direct experience basic to the development of concepts and generalizations. This often results in the use of stereotypes sterile and excentric[2].

Et, à partir de ses importantes recherches, Berenice M. Casper a dressé plusieurs tableaux concernant la portée et le déroulement de l'éducation géographique de l'élève. Ces tableaux indiquent à quel niveau scolaire on doit enseigner telle ou telle notion géographique. Ils permettent donc de raccrocher à ces concepts le vocabulaire approprié et d'assurer par là plus d'efficacité aux connaissances transmises.

En 1962, Mme Debesse-Arviset publiait les conclusions d'une importante enquête[3] sur la notion d'espace géographique effectuée auprès des jeunes élèves français de 10-12 ans. Ses conclusions portent sur les causes des déficiences en géographie, les remèdes et montrent, à la fin, l'utilité de l'enquête pour l'observation du travail profond de l'intelligence. « Car, affirme-t-elle, la notion-mère d'espace géographique conditionne le développement ultérieur de l'esprit et révèle son degré d'organisation; elle mesure vraiment la valeur intellectuelle : c'est sur elle, et sur d'autres notions-mères, que devraient porter l'observation et l'orientation pour lesquelles on cherche actuellement des critères[4]. »

Et cette enquête, au dire de Mme Debesse-Arviset, « montre la nocivité des mots appris et incompris, qui se chargent de représentations absurdes faute d'en pouvoir contenir d'assimilables[5] ». Et encore : « Toutes les questions de l'enquête ont permis de déceler une déficience, parfois peu croyable, du vocabulaire des élèves[6]. » Enfin, parmi les remèdes que ce pédagogue recommande pour mettre fin à cette importante lacune, la méthode d'apprentissage actuelle des notions à travers la terminologie est remise en question : « ... l'acquisition du vocabulaire géographique doit être méthodique et systématiquement surveillée, moins par des exercices verbaux que par l'attention du sens que l'enfant donne aux mots qu'il emploie[7]. »

Par ailleurs, chez nous, en 1964, Maurice Saint-Yves publiait dans les *Cahiers de géographie de Québec*[8] les résultats d'une autre enquête effectuée auprès des élèves de huitième année de la ville de Québec. Cette enquête voulait vérifier le comportement des élèves en face de la géographie générale. À propos du vocabulaire des élèves, Maurice Saint-Yves écrit :

---

[2] *Ibidem*, p. 237.
[3] M.-L. DEBESSE-ARVISET, « Enquête sur la formation de la notion d'espace géographique », *Le courrier de la recherche pédagogique* », 16 (1962), 27-55.
[4] *Ibidem*, p. 47.
[5] *Ibidem*, p. 49.
[6] *Ibidem*, p. 50.
[7] *Ibidem*, p. 53.
[8] M. SAINT-YVES, « Contribution à la pédagogie de la géographie : une enquête chez les élèves de huitième année », *Cahiers de géographie de Québec*, 8, 15 (1963-64), 139-148.

Nous avons vu que 90% des sujets de notre enquête ne peuvent définir le mot *paysage* dans son sens géographique. De même que pour le mot
relief, ils comprennent le sens populaire du terme et sans doute
conservent-ils ce sens dans les textes géographiques qu'ils ont sous les
yeux. Voilà qui explique bien des confusions absurdes relevées dans des
copies d'élèves même beaucoup plus âgés que ceux dont il est question
ici[9].

Plus récemment, en 1972, Dennis Milburn faisait connaître les
résultats de son enquête effectuée auprès des élèves de Londres[10] sur
le vocabulaire géographique et les concepts véhiculés par lui. « The
average overall rate of attempt in the primary school was that 44.47%
of the terms were defined[11]. » Plus loin, Dennis Milburn affirme que
de nombreux termes de base de première importance restent encore
incompris dans les premières années de l'école secondaire[12]. Et
quand l'auteur du rapport fait la synthèse de ses observations sur le
vocabulaire géographique des sujets soumis aux tests, tant à l'élémentaire qu'au secondaire, il conclut en disant :

> In general it could be deduced from the tests that, by the end of each
> main period of general education (i.e. at 11 and 16) pupils in the sample
> know approximately 62% of the geographical terms which are used in
> schools. However, they vary considerably in their ability to use them as
> aids to their own development[13].

Un tel pourcentage à propos d'une acquisition « approximative » du
vocabulaire géographique ne permet certes pas de conclure à un enseignement efficace, loin de là.

Deux Américains faisaient, en 1975, des constatations sembla-
bles à partir d'un test administré à 1 689 élèves de cinquième année[14] :

> Questions based on physical geography were the most difficult for
> these students. For example, 84 percent of them did not understand the
> physical geography principle associated with directional flow of a river
> contained in question 4. Other questions pertaining to the effects of differ-
> ential heating and cooling of land and water bodies and the erosional
> potential of running water, which are not contained in this article, were
> very difficult. Certain physical terms such as *plain* and *continent* were
> missed frequently, and large numbers of students failed to recognize cer-
> tain land masses and large bodies of water[15].

Ces résultats d'enquêtes plus importantes et ceux que de nombreux autres éducateurs[16] ont obtenus mettent en évidence la consta-

---

[9]   *Ibidem*, p. 147.
[10]   D. MILBURN, « Children's Vocabulary », dans N. GRAVES (éd.), *New Movements in the Study and Teaching of Geography*, London, Temple Smith, 1972,
p. 107-120.
[11]   *Ibidem*, p. 114.
[12]   *Ibidem*, p. 117.
[13]   *Ibidem*, p. 117.
[14]   N. C. BETTIS et G. A. MANSON, « An assessment of the Geographic Learning
of Fifth Grade Students in Michigan », *The Journal of Geography*, 74, 1 (1976), 16-24.
[15]   *Ibidem*, p. 17.
[16]   La revue *The Journal of Geography*, entre autres, contient de nombreux
témoignages qui corroborent ces assertions.

tation du peu d'efficacité de l'enseignement géographique dispensé aux jeunes élèves. Inutile d'insister davantage pour faire valoir alors la nécessité de se pencher sur le problème, de l'étudier en profondeur et d'en chercher toutes les implications afin d'assurer à l'enseignement de la géographie cette efficacité à laquelle on est en droit de s'attendre.

III.— LA DIDACTIQUE ET LE VOCABULAIRE GÉOGRAPHIQUE

Parler du problème de l'enseignement du vocabulaire géographique situe notre article dans le domaine de la didactique, plus spécialement dans le champ de recherche de la géographie. Toute science, nous l'avons déjà dit, doit être transmise dans son intégrité avec le maximum d'assurance que l'enseignement donné est perçu correctement du sujet. Or, c'est la didactique, matière englobante, qui, parce qu'elle puise aux sources de la psychologie, de la pédagogie, de la méthodologie et, ici, de la géographie, assure une meilleure qualité à l'enseignement transmis.

La didactique, peut-on dire, est une science auxiliaire de la pédagogie, relative aux méthodes les plus propres à faire acquérir telle ou telle notion, celle d'*occupation du territoire* par exemple. Elle est fondamentalement une réflexion sur une discipline, ici la géographie, en vue de l'enseignement de cette discipline. Mais, cette préoccupation essentielle de la didactique la confronte constamment avec des problèmes d'ordre psychologique qui surgissent normalement chez l'être en situation d'apprentissage. La didactique, en conséquence, exige du maître une double formation, formation dans sa discipline et formation en psychologie de l'éducation. De plus, il doit orienter son activité intellectuelle vers l'application pédagogique.

En somme, par didactique, il faut entendre un processus qui vise à amener l'élève à acquérir telle ou telle notion, telle opération ou telle technique de travail[17]. Dans presque tous les programmes scolaires, la géographie incluse, les tâches de la didactique sont définies en termes de notions à acquérir. On dira alors que l'élève connaît bien la notion de *paysage* ou celle de *ville* ou les lois qui régissent la vie d'un cours d'eau, etc. Donc, en étudiant la nature, l'objet et les méthodes de travail de la géographie, la didactique nous introduit dans une démarche, ou plus précisément un certain mode d'analyse des phénomènes de l'enseignement de la géographie qui doit assurer l'aspect cognitif et l'aspect éducatif de cette discipline.

---

[17]   G. Palmade, *Les méthodes en pédagogie*, Paris, P.U.F., 1971, Collection « Que sais-je ?, no 572, p. 39.

IV. — LES PRINCIPES D'UTILISATION DE LA NOMENCLATURE GÉOGRAPHIQUE

Afin d'améliorer la qualité de la transmission des connaissances géographiques, nous tenterons de poser quelques principes généraux d'utilisation de la nomenclature en géographie, soit la terminologie et la choronymie. En effet, « le caractère spatial de l'optique géographique amène le géographe à manier un vocabulaire composé, non seulement de termes GÉNÉTIQUES destinés à désigner des phénomènes ou des types de paysage, mais aussi des termes SPÉCIFIQUES qui désignent des éléments uniques, traduits, en toponymie, par des noms propres[18] ».

Dès qu'on aborde le sujet de la nomenclature en géographie, le problème de la mémorisation surgit immédiatement. Parlons-en tout de suite, puisqu'il le faut ! Heureusement, on peut affirmer sans crainte de se tromper que l'enseignement de la géographie tend incontestablement à développer, entre autres facultés, la mémoire; et cela est très positif en soi. Autrefois, c'était hélas sinon son seul but, du moins presque son seul résultat ! Une utilisation pertinente de la mémoire deviendra donc ici un second moyen proposé pour améliorer l'acquisition des concepts à travers la nomenclature géographique. Parmi les formes de mémoire possibles, la géographie intéresse surtout les suivantes : la mémoire verbale et la mémoire visuelle.

L'enseignement de la géographie développe d'abord la mémoire verbale par la force même des choses : en effet, comment faire de la géographie sans s'imposer de retenir un minimum de noms, ne fût-ce que comme jalons ou comme repères ! D'ailleurs, une géographie sans nom, sans nomenclature, serait proprement un non-sens. Mais il faudra veiller à ne pas retomber dans les erreurs d'autrefois. L'espace géographique n'est pas un espace indéterminé, amorphe et anonyme, c'est un espace caractérisé qui a un nom unique. C'est pourquoi, il est nécessaire que l'écolier apprenne à nommer cet espace, il doit retenir un certain nombre de noms propres qui sont les points de repères précis dans l'étude de la géographie. Il est évident que le professeur ne peut à l'occasion d'une étude régionale, par exemple, répéter et localiser indéfiniment les mêmes noms; ceux-ci doivent être appris et retenus une fois pour toutes. Il y a donc une choronymie indispensable, mais le problème n'est pas là, il est davantage dans le choix et dans le volume de mots à confier à la mémoire de l'enfant.

Autrefois, on ne faisait que de la nomenclature : des listes interminables de noms de montagnes, de fleuves, de villes, etc., enseignement ennuyeux, certes, mais, on le reconnaît aujourd'hui, pas complètement inutile. En effet, on assurait la possession en quelque

---

[18]   L.-E. HAMELIN et H. DORION, *Réflexions méthodologiques sur le langage géographique*, Québec, Université Laval, 1966, Publications du Groupe d'étude de choronymie et de terminologie géographique n° 1, p. 39.

sorte définitive "d'un savoir sec mais précis[19]», selon l'expression d'Omer Tulippe (1954), et l'on créait des associations d'idées indestructibles que le temps lui-même ne parvenait pas à entamer. Mais, selon Ozouf (1937), «cette méthode comportait trop d'efforts perdus et l'acquisition de trop de notions inutiles. Elle sacrifiait à l'excès l'intelligence des faits à la connaissance abstraite[20]».

Par une réaction bien compréhensible, mais sans doute excessive, contre ces errements, on a réduit dans la suite la nomenclature à rien ou presque rien. Autre erreur! Car, comme déjà dit, la choronymie doit servir de jalons, de repères précis, de supports. Ceux qui la condamnent, au dire de R. Ozouf (1937), «ne font qu'ériger en principe leur propre ignorance ou la paresse de leur mémoire verbale[21]».

Mais les élèves n'auront pas à retenir toute la nomenclature utilisée dans les différentes leçons. On fera un tri. On conservera l'essentiel, c'est-à-dire le bagage de choronymes permettant la localisation des faits géographiques importants et, éventuellement, les termes du vocabulaire de base. D'ailleurs le fait de savoir identifier et localiser excite l'élève à connaître davantage.

Outre la mémoire des mots, l'enseignement de la géographie doit aussi et surtout développer la mémoire visuelle ou mémoire des formes, le mot *forme* étant à considérer dans son sens le plus large et englobant tous les phénomènes géographiques. Cette mémoire visuelle joue, en effet, un grand rôle, particulièrement dans les exercices d'observation. Le fait géographique est un fait visuel, il a une forme et une couleur, il suggère à l'esprit une image. C'est dans la perception de ce fait que la mémoire visuelle intervient. S'il est vrai que percevoir c'est en grande partie se souvenir, la perception d'un fait géographique sera d'autant plus rapide et complète que l'élève aura dans sa mémoire une plus grande variété d'images visuelles, sources de comparaisons nombreuses. Cela est particulièrement vrai en géographie physique où l'écolier doit s'habituer à retenir des «formes», forme d'un relief, d'un paysage, d'une région, d'un continent. La mémoire visuelle s'exerce aussi bien à partir de l'observation directe ou indirecte. Convenablement exercée, elle facilite énormément le travail de l'intelligence car elle permet d'avoir une vision claire des faits dont on parle.

À ce sujet, Ozouf (1937) ajoute encore :

> Ainsi, vouloir supprimer ou réduire exagérément la nomenclature serait enlever à la géographie une grande partie de ses fondements et une grande partie de son utilité pratique. Mais on la réduira au minimum en s'en tenant aux faits géographiques essentiels et en abandonnant les termes techniques ou prétentieux[22].

---

[19] O. TULIPPE, *Méthodologie de la géographie*, Liège, Sciences et Lettres, 1954, p. 40.

[20] R. OZOUF, *Vade-Mecum pour l'enseignement de la géographie*, Paris, Nathan, 1937, p. 52.

[21] *Ibidem*, p. 53.

[22] *Ibidem*, p. 55.

L'acquisition, solide, il va sans dire, de ce minimum sera facilité par l'emploi de procédés méthodologiques appropriés. Autrement dit, il faut faciliter autant que possible le travail de mémorisation. Mais au lieu d'utiliser les moyens mémotechniques puérils et enfantins d'autrefois, on basera la mémorisation sur des données géographiques d'observation et de raisonnement. Ou bien, on accompagnera le terme à retenir de quelques explications qui aideront à fixer le mot. Bref, on appellera à son aide les moyens « intelligents », de façon qu'autant que possible, le mot et la chose marchent de pair dans l'esprit. « Bien entendu, il ne s'agit pas de donner une définition abstraite à l'élève qui risquerait de ne pas voir ou de mal voir, à travers elle, l'objet que l'on veut définir[23] ».

Soit dit en passant, le problème des définitions en géographie est le même que pour bien des branches du savoir. Commencer une leçon par débiter une définition, puis l'expliquer est un procédé de facilité, outre qu'il est anti-méthodologique. C'est le livre qui, souvent, procède de la sorte; et rien ne l'excuse d'ailleurs ! Car, pourquoi le livre ne s'inspirerait-il pas dans sa présentation des exigences de la méthodologie ? On répondra qu'il est le syllabus qui a pour unique but de remettre la matière sous les yeux des élèves. Le livre devrait toujours suivre le même ordre que celui de la leçon, à savoir : commencer par faire apparaître la notion dans ses différents aspects ou modalités, puis arriver de proche en proche à édifier, à construire, mot par mot, ou idée par idée, la définition, celle-ci venant après, comme couronnement de l'exposé.

On le constate donc, quel que soit le sujet d'étude en géographie, la mémoire doit sans cesse intervenir pour enregistrer les faits, les termes et les notions. Encore faut-il que ce travail se fasse selon les lois psychologiques de la mémoire, c'est-à-dire en respectant la nature même de cette faculté. En examinant ce point de vue, nous pourrons peut-être définir les normes didactiques de ce recours constant à la mémoire dans l'enseignement de la géographie.

Le psychologue Paul Fraisse (1962) dans un article[24] a résumé, avec un sens psychologique et pédagogique très sûr, les conditions d'une bonne mémorisation. Selon cet auteur, quatre lois sont à retenir :

1.   Mémoriser est le résultat d'une activité organisatrice et tout ce qui favorisera cette activité sera bénéfique pour la mémoire;

2.   La mémorisation s'obtient plus économiquement quand on introduit des intervalles convenables entre les efforts consécutifs d'acquisition (Loi de Jost);

3.   Apprendre à mémoriser, c'est apprendre à organiser. Ce que nous devons faire c'est apprendre à l'enfant à apprendre, c'est-à-dire apprendre à lier, à organiser les données éparses et ce qui pourra alors être acquis, ce sera la technique même de liaison et de mémorisation;

---

23   *Ibidem*, p. 57.
24   P. Fraisse, « Plaidoyer pour la mémoire », *Enfance*, 4-5 1962, 324-327.

4. Il n'y a mémorisation que s'il y a, non seulement le désir d'apprendre, mais si ce que l'on apprend s'insère dans l'expérience vécue du sujet.

On peut donc de suite déduire de ces lois que la mémorisation à l'école doit être un acte d'intelligence et de jugement. On ne mémorise pas pour le simple fait de mémoriser. À la base de chaque mémorisation il doit y avoir un but, une préoccupation de conserver cet acquis pour un avenir plus ou moins lointain. D'après l'auteur que nous venons de citer, « le rôle propre de la mémoire sera toujours beaucoup plus de prévoir que de revoir ». L'élève ne saisit pas toujours cette relation dans l'étude d'une matière comme la géographie. Ainsi, il ne voit pas parfois que les notions de géographie générale qu'il apprend dans le temps présent lui seront bien précieuses dans les années suivantes pour comprendre les faits de géographie régionale. Il y a donc dans l'enseignement de cette discipline une gradation dans les notions à mémoriser.

Cette gradation suppose une organisation des connaissances que l'élève doit comprendre et retenir afin d'y intégrer les notions nouvelles qui se présenteront à lui. Selon la première et la troisième lois que nous avons citées, la mémorisation doit donc se faire dans le cadre de cette organisation et il serait suspect d'imposer la mémorisation d'une notion isolée sans liens fonctionnels avec ce qui précède et ce qui suit. On devine que ces lois sont la condamnation de cette géographie énumérative d'autrefois qui ne mettait en oeuvre qu'une sorte de mémoire mécanique.

Tout cela permettra à l'élève de se faire une image précise des faits. Et dans tous les cas, la nécessité d'une description exacte s'impose; il faut éviter le verbiage sans fondement, sans base, sans intérêt. Pour l'élève, les termes n'ont de valeur que quand ils sont mis en rapport avec des phénomènes qu'il peut observer. Bref, la description doit être présentée en des termes concrets, pittoresques, évocateurs. Ainsi apparaît la nécessité des cartes, croquis, cartogrammes, photos, diagrammes, chiffres, échantillons de produits, moulage de toute matière.

Pour faciliter la tâche de l'enseignement de la nomenclature, il est recommandé de recourir, mais sans abus, à la signification des mots en géographie, surtout des mots d'origine étrangère. Ce procédé met d'ailleurs parfois sur la piste d'une explication géographique du genre de celle préconisée ci-dessus.

En géographie, le travail de description et celui d'explication nécessitent l'emploi d'un vocabulaire technique. Toutefois, avec les jeunes élèves, il ne faut pas abuser des termes techniques; il faut en limiter le nombre au strict nécessaire, tout en restant fidèle au terme propre. Leur emploi n'est permis qu'à la condition de s'être assuré que les termes sont bien compris des élèves et qu'ils correspondent à une réalité dans leur esprit. Il faut en régler le nombre d'après l'âge et le degré d'évolution des enfants en cause.

Par ailleurs, puisqu'il est question de terminologie, il n'est pas inutile de signaler qu'il faut bannir de l'enseignement élémentaire l'abus, voire simplement l'usage de termes derrière lesquels il n'y a rien et qui masquent souvent notre ignorance; par exemple, la *surimposition*, l'*antécédence*, etc. Il faut aussi condamner sévèrement les professeurs qui, pour éblouir leur auditoire, embarrassent les leçons de géographie de termes techniques ronflants empruntés à d'autres sciences : ce sont là des attitudes qui risquent de dégoûter les élèves ou d'en faire de pauvres pédants. Néanmoins, tous les conseils, toutes les exhortations ci-dessus tendant à réduire le nombre de vocables techniques, ne doivent pas être considérés comme exprimant le voeu de conserver la géographie dans un état mineur par rapport aux autres sciences. Au contraire ! L'enseignement géographique, à cet égard aussi, doit être hissé au niveau des autres enseignements. Cet effort doit débuter dans les classes inférieures et progresser dans la suite quand les élèves passent dans les années d'études postérieures.

À propos de nomenclature, rappelons ici trois recommandations faites par l'UNESCO (1952). D'abord celle où, après avoir dit que dans de nombreux pays c'est vers onze ans que les enfants abordent l'étude des autres nations et pays : « À cet âge, il convient de recommander les récits sur la vie et le travail dans les régions caractéristiques du globe ainsi que sur les expéditions de grands explorateurs et de voyageurs modernes. De telles études géographiques permettront à l'enfant de glaner une gerbe sans cesse plus fournie de faits significatifs et de termes géographiques utiles[25]. » La seconde recommandation s'adresse ensuite aux enseignants pour leur rappeler, au sujet de la choronymie :

> En général, il vaut mieux s'abstenir de citer des noms et d'utiliser des atlas jusqu'à ce qu'on ait fait revivre le lieu que l'on souhaite évoquer. L'élève ne saurait se contenter d'apprendre à repérer un endroit sur un atlas et prétendre ensuite qu'il connaît la provenance des divers objets : de toute évidence, une telle connaissance serait tout à fait illusoire[26].

La troisième recommandation, elle, rejoint ce que nous disions plus haut à propos des élèves de 9 à 12 ans :

> Au cours de cette phase, l'enfant dont la mémoire demeure bonne et dont l'intelligence s'est affinée, est en général capable d'assimiler une bonne partie des termes employés en géographie dans les définitions et les descriptions. Ce travail exige peut-être un certain nombre d'exercices mécaniques, mais en enrichissant son vocabulaire, l'enfant apprend à se montrer plus précis et parvient à suivre les leçons de géographie d'un niveau plus élevé[27].

En fait, chacune des fonctions mentales joue son rôle dans l'apprentissage de la géographie, mais l'appel à la mémoire est inévitable

---

[25]   UNESCO, L'enseignement de la géographie. Petit guide à l'usage des maîtres, dans *Vers une compréhension internationale*, n° X, Paris, Unesco, 1952, p. 23.

[26]   *Ibidem*, p. 25.

[27]   *Ibidem*, p. 27.

parce que la géographie la plus élémentaire suppose une nomenclature localisée. Les noms de fleuves, de massifs montagneux ou de villes servent de soubassement à l'étude géographique elle-même. Rappelons-le encore, ce qu'il faut proscrire, c'est l'abus de la nomenclature qui encombe la pensée et en paralyse l'activité; c'est aussi de réduire cet enseignement à n'être qu'un exercice de mémoire, une récitation de mots et de faits. Un éducateur sensé comprend bien que si l'intelligence n'est pas la mémoire, il n'y a pas de travail intellectuel possible sans l'appui de souvenirs précis, autrement dit pas de culture sans contenu, en géographie comme ailleurs. On entend souvent dire que, dans l'enseignement élémentaire, la terminologie et la choronymie tiennent souvent encore trop de place. C'est probable, mais l'expérience montre que, souvent aussi, une mémoire d'écolier peut, faute de soins, être aussi pauvre que confuse : les examens en apportent des preuves affligeantes.

L'observation est l'antidote de la mémoire livresque et l'aliment d'une mémoire intelligemment exercée. Loin de se réduire à l'enregistrement passif des choses perçues ou à une curiosité papillonnante, elle met en oeuvre toutes les activités de l'esprit. « Observer, c'est penser pour s'efforcer de connaître[28]. » L'enseignement géographique permet d'entraîner l'enfant à une observation de plus en plus méthodique et précise des phénomènes naturels et humains de la surface de la terre. L'étude du milieu local en particulier, offre pour cela une richesse inépuisable[29]. L'élève y prend peu à peu une attitude comparable, toutes proportions gardées, à celle du géographe au cours de ses recherches. Cela suppose un long et patient entraînement car si rien ne paraît aussi facile que d'observer, rien n'est plus difficile que de bien observer.

Dans son enquête sur la notion d'espace géographique, M.-L. Debesse-Arviset (1962) propose cinq remèdes contre les déficiences constatées chez les élèves à propos du vocabulaire géographique et de leurs causes. C'est à un changement de méthode d'enseignement de la géographie qu'elle invite les professeurs[30] et nous y retrouvons cet aspect de l'observation dont il vient d'être question.

1. D'abord, partir de l'observation d'exemples concrets, au lieu de définitions mal comprises et de raisonnements déductifs qui faussent souvent l'esprit;

2. Prendre conscience qu'il faut peu à peu, lentement mais continuellement, former les notions-mères essentielles au développement de l'esprit, que c'est le but primordial de l'accroissement du savoir;

---

[28] m.-L. DEBESSE-ARVISET et M. DEBESSE, dans M. SORRE, La géographie, Cahiers de pédagogie moderne, Paris, Bourrelier, 1953, p. 35.

[29] Voir M.-L. DEBESSE-ARVISET, L'environnement à l'école, une révolution pédagogique, Paris, P.U.F., 1973, Collection « S.U.P. », n°42, 136 pages.

[30] M.-L. DEBESSE-ARVISET, Enquête sur la formation de la notion d'espace géographique, p. 52.

3. Employer pour la formation des notions essentielles les exercices de recherche, d'application, de réalisations manuelles, remplaçant les exposés faits au bureau et les récitations faites au tableau. En géométrie, l'essentiel est la démonstration et le problème d'application; en géographie, il consiste à savoir localiser, observer, rapprocher les faits pour les expliquer;

4. La localisation doit être au premier plan de la leçon de géographie, le point de départ de l'exposé ou de la recherche, le point de départ de l'interrogation, l'objet de nombreux exercices, la conclusion de tous. La localisation sur une carte se complète, pour les pays éloignés, par la localisation sur le globe; car les perspectives vraies se rétablissent sur celui-ci;

5. Enfin, l'acquisition du vocabulaire géographique doit être méthodique et systématiquement surveillée, moins par des exercices verbaux que par l'attention du sens que l'enfant donne aux mots qu'il emploie. Les noms qui désignent des objets concrets nouveaux pour lui ne sauraient être acquis qu'accompagnés de la vue, de la manipulation, de l'utilisation de ces objets. Pour les termes à l'acception différente de celle du langage courant, il est nécessaire non seulement d'attirer l'attention sur cette différence, mais d'exercer les élèves à les employer souvent dans leur sens précis et scientifique. Il faut aussi se méfier des images. Certainement, nous devons éveiller l'imagination par des descriptions, mais que de visions fausses nous provoquons parfois !

Dans son ouvrage sur la mémoire, J.-C. Filloux (1969) dit qu'il faut envisager la répétition comme un facteur de l'acquisition volontaire : « C'est surtout lui qui influe dans l'acquisition de la mémoire-habitude, puisque les automatismes moteurs sont le fruit de la répétition[31]. » Cette assertion s'avère des plus utiles quand il s'agit de présenter la nomenclature géographique à des élèves de 9-12 ans. Le professeur doit donc employer le plus souvent possible les termes et les choronymes qu'il désire faire assimiler. C'est là, d'ailleurs, une loi de l'apprentissage du langage : « Plus un mot, par exemple, est fréquent dans la langue, plus souvent il a été entendu ou lu par les individus qui pratiquent cette langue, et plus facilement il est reconnu à l'audition ou à la lecture, évoqué en réponse à une série de stimuli quelconques, appris dans un groupe de mots ou deviné dans une phrase incomplète[32]. »

Un autre aspect de l'enseignement du vocabulaire géographique sur lequel on ne saurait trop insister est l'exactitude des termes. Parce que la géographie est aussi description, il faut décrire exactement, trouver les mots justes. L'UNESCO (1949) le rappelle fort justement aux professeurs[33]. En effet, décrire suppose la connaissance d'un mi-

---

[31]   J.-C. FILLOUX, *La mémoire*, Paris, P.U.F., 1969, Collection « Que sais-je ? » n° 350, p. 78.

[32]   J.-F. LE NY, « Apprentissage », *Encyclopaedia Universalis*, 2 (1973), 175.

[33]   UNESCO, « L'enseignement de la géographie : quelques conseils et suggestions », dans *Vers la compréhension internationale*, Paris, Unesco, 1949, p. 26.

nimum de termes géographiques. Un élève sortant d'un cours complet de géographie ne devrait pas, d'après cet organisme international, trébucher devant les termes géographiques de son temps, car la science et la nomenclature géographique évoluent, et des termes nouveaux apparaissent toujours pour des concepts nouveaux. Au passage, on fera remarquer aux enfants les différences entre la *terminologie locale*, toujours intéressante, pittoresque même, riche d'observations ancestrales et d'expériences pratiques, mais dont il ne faut pas abuser, car elle est souvent restreinte et incompréhensible aux autres, la *terminologie nationale* admise par les géographes du pays et, enfin, une certaine *terminologie internationale* que l'on devrait le plus possible adopter; ce sont le plus souvent des termes savants devenus classiques et qui peuvent être utiles pour des phénomènes qui n'existent pas dans tous les pays (fjords), ou qui évoquent tout un paysage (karst); évidemment, la liste de ces termes ne doit pas excéder la mémoire des enfants.

L'on ne conçoit pas plus des géographes qui ne parleraient pas le même langage que des chimistes qui n'utiliseraient pas les mêmes symboles. De là, le conseil suivant aux professeurs : utilisez un langage commun rendant le vocabulaire cohérent, appelez les choses par leur nom, mais aussi ordonnez la description, bâtissez un plan et colorez, non pas platement, mais en termes géographiques choisis et exacts. En attendant que le vocabulaire de base de la géographie soit établi, les professeurs de géographie d'une même régionale pourraient s'entendre pour faire assimiler aux élèves d'un même niveau une terminologie à peu près identique. Les publications pourraient en cela jouer un rôle de premier ordre.

Dans le même ordre d'idées, on peut aussi dire qu'avant d'ajouter un terme au vocabulaire géographique des élèves, il faut s'assurer que ce mot répond vraiment à une nécessité, soit immédiate, soit relativement proche. Il n'est pas à conseiller d'introduire des termes géographiques qui ne seront pas fréquemment employés, puisqu'on peut répondre aux besoins éventuels au moyen de brèves expressions descriptives. Les élèves ne se soucieront généralement pas d'apprendre des termes trop spécialisés, dans les cas de ce genre, et les rares étudiants qui se hasarderont à employer les termes recommandés pourront ne pas être compris[34].

En somme, on peut retenir cinq normes didactiques plus importantes découlant des conditions d'une bonne mémorisation en vue de la transmission des connaissances à travers le vocabulaire géographique :

1. La mémorisation doit se faire dans une préoccupation d'utiliser cet acquis dans l'avenir;

2. La mémorisation exige une organisation et une gradation des connaissances et du vocabulaire qui les véhicule;

---

[34] UNESCO, *L'emploi des langues vernaculaires dans l'enseignement*, Paris, Unesco, 1953, p. 76.

3.   La mémorisation suppose un choix des termes utiles;
4.   La mémorisation exige la répétition;
5.   La mémorisation doit faire appel à l'activité de l'élève.

Comme conclusion à cette partie de notre article nous proposons les six suggestions suivantes qui résument les expériences tentées par Z. A. Thralls (1958) dans l'enseignement de la nomenclature géographique. Ces suggestions résument et complètent bien ce que nous en avons dit plus haut.

1.   Introduce each new word or concept as needed in meaningful discussion.
2.   Use the new word orally as often as the opportunity arises so that the pupils become familiar with the sound symbols and with its meaning in relation to geography.
3.   Provide accurate concrete imagery of the word through the use of the local landscape, pictures, diagrams, sketches, specimens, and so forth.
4.   Write the word on the blackboard as you discuss it.
5.   Provide opportunities for the pupils to read textbook sentences containing the word or phrase.
6.   Ask questions which require the use of the word in oral and written situations[35].

V. — CONCLUSION : LE VOCABULAIRE GÉOGRAPHIQUE ET LA VIE QUOTIDIENNE

Affirmer que les enfants vivent et vivront bien davantage encore à l'âge adulte dans un monde dominé par les applications de la science en général et de la géographie en particulier aux activités humaines de toutes catégories est une vérité d'évidence.

C'est donc la notion même de culture qui est en cause, car l'éducation, dès l'école élémentaire, doit s'efforcer avec lucidité et persévérance, d'une part, de doter l'enfant de moyens de pensée et d'action qui l'aideront à vivre tout en sauvegardant sa liberté intérieure et sa dignité d'homme; d'autre part, de transmettre un héritage, une culture, mais aussi les moyens d'accroître celui-là et de jouir de celle-ci en l'enrichissant.

Quelle application peut-on faire de ces idées lorsqu'on parle de didactique de la géographie ? Les méthodes modernes d'éducation en géographie se fondent sur la psychologie et l'évolution de la croissance mentale et affective. Elles tiennent compte des conditions de la vie qui ont rendu l'enfant plus précoce face à son environnement, à l'image de ces plantes dont on raccourcit le cycle végétatif en les forçant, les rendant ainsi plus vulnérables à tout ce qui menace leur intégrité biologique.

Nous savons que les méthodes nouvelles en géographie sont difficiles à employer et à pratiquer surtout. Vouloir que les enfants soient les artisans de leur propre savoir, prôner la pédagogie de l'inté-

---

[35]   Z. A. THRALLS, *The Teaching of Geography*, New York, Appleton-Century-Crofts, 1958, p. 203.

rêt, les méthodes actives, le travail de redécouverte, l'expérimentation, l'enseignement individualisé, l'étude du milieu, les activités dirigées, le travail par équipes, l'éducation à la responsabilité, demande du temps, si l'on veut concilier l'acquisition solide des connaissances géographiques indispensables avec la mise en valeur des aptitudes individuelles et le traitement des caractères. Il ne s'agit pas là, du reste, d'une revendication des partisans des méthodes d'enseignement, uniquement, mais bien des conséquences sur le travail scolaire en géographie, de l'évolution accélérée de la science et des progrès de la technique. La vie professionnelle, demain, demandera plus de capacités, plus d'efforts intellectuels, plus de possibilités d'adaptation.

Apprendre ne suffit pas : le livre, la bibliothèque, les publications spécialisées, voire la radiophonie et la télévision, permettent à chacun de compléter en tout temps, à son gré et dans tous les domaines touchés par la géographie, les connaissances acquises à l'école. D'où l'importance d'avoir acquis un vocabulaire de base en géographie que l'on sait manier intelligemment et dont on sait faire une application adéquate dans les différentes situations de la vie quotidienne. Avoir des concepts clairs, pouvoir identifier, localiser, décrire, expliquer les divers phénomènes géographiques suppose une nomenclature appropriée, assez vaste pour couvrir leurs caractéristiques.

Éduquer, aujourd'hui, c'est apprendre à apprendre, apprendre à penser, apprendre à agir. L'école ne peut plus vivre en circuit fermé et se borner à faire acquérir un certain nombre de connaissances géographiques en vue surtout de préparer à des examens de caractère formel le plus souvent.

Si l'école ne veut pas accentuer son divorce avec la vie, elle doit modifier ses méthodes et, conjointement, l'esprit de ses programmes de géographie et le contenu de ceux-ci. Le développement de l'enfant ne dépendra pas seulement de sa possibilité d'éducation; il est aussi relié à la quantité de matière géographique couverte et à la façon de présenter une situation d'apprentissage. La compréhension de la plupart des termes géographiques peut s'améliorer si elle est soumise à une étude intensive et présentée dans des situations variées. L'expression verbale correcte en géographie doit être encouragée pour que, jointe à une expérience vivante, elle aide à consolider l'apprentissage des notions géographiques. L'acquisition des concepts et celle d'un vocabulaire vivant sont des aspects complémentaires du processus de développement intellectuel dans l'éducation géographique.

THE LONGITUDINAL ASPECT OF EVALUATION IN GEOGRAPHY

GERALD T. RIMMINGTON
Mount Allison University

In visiting and observing the practice in many Canadian high schools one is led to the conclusion that, whatever the age and stage of development of the student, evaluation is the one aspect of a teacher's work that tends to remain fairly constant throughout. It is assumed that curriculum and methods of teaching will show evidence of changing emphases and increasing sophistication as the adolescent progresses through the school, but that evaluation methods will remain virtually the same. The question that one wants to ask and to explore, therefore, is whether evaluation techniques should not show a progression similar to other aspects of school work.

In the beginning, it has to be admired that our psychologists and measurement experts have not encouraged us to think in terms of changes within instruments over time. For instance, to take an example of a good recently written textbook, Gage and Berliner's *Educational Psychology* (1975), there are four excellent chapters on various aspects of evaluation, but there is no mention anywhere of increasing sophistication within measurement instruments from grade VII to XII. This is undoubtedly because measurement specialists are mainly interested in perfecting standardized tests that, when administered at any level, will, by their very constancy, show the point that a student has reached in one or more aspects of the continuum of human development.

Despite the predilections of measurement specialists, which are perfectly valid in the case of standardized tests, there is perhaps a case for treating day-to-day evaluation by teachers in a different manner. The teacher faced with the task of evaluating the work of a high school grade is not too concerned, in that particular exercise, with relating to the work of other grades, except in terms of increasing sophistication, both in curriculum and human development. It does not matter very much that there is no standardization. The important thing is that the measurement instruments used shall be appropriate to the particular group of students that is in process of being evaluated

To establish a principle, however, is one thing; the translation of that principle into classroom practice is another matter. It is not easy in the case of geography (or any of the sciences which have social aspects), for this is a subject area in which there is no clearly defined and agreed upon hierarchy of objectives and teaching strategies. It is a matter of opinion, for instance, whether we teach the geographical principles of the weather systems experienced in Canada in grade VII or XII, or whether the student is confronted by West African cocoa production at the age of twelve or seventeen.

The situation is chaotic enough, but not quite as bad as it may seem to be, for every curriculum developer in geography has at the back of his mind some concern for increasing sophistication, so that what is being taught at one level builds upon the work of preceding years. Similarly, every teacher has at the back of his mind some notions as to what are appropriate evaluation instruments at particular levels. Most would accept, for instance, that the formal essay is less appropriate at the lower grades than the higher ones, and that oral forms of testing are more appropriate with less literate than highly literate students.

There are two dimensions to the development of curricula, which have relevance to the development of evaluation techniques, and which represent significant differences of emphasis. There are, firstly, those who approach the problem from the viewpoint of curriculum theory. To take but one of those theorists, Jerome Bruner has hypothesized that there is no subject matter to be taught and evaluated that is inherently more appropriate to one grade level than another. He stresses that there is no fundamental difference between one level of learning and another, and that the small child should be doing in a less sophisticated manner what the research worker is doing at his own level. Hence Bruner envisages a spiral curriculum in which there is continuity and repetition. Within each section of the spiral (representing a year of schooling) there is a need to return to the same principles, in a more advanced form suitable to the growing awareness of the student (Bruner, 1960 and Rimmington, 1969).

It is not difficult to see that in a subject like geography a spiral curriculum may be developed with relative ease. Elsewhere the writer has noted :

> one may visualize immediately a number of strands which run through succeeding levels. The construction of maps, for instance, begins with the simple sketch map and leads through stages to the appreciation of mathematically constructed map projections. The study of urban phenomena may begin with simple observations of the distribution of shops in the immediate vicinity of school and home, continue through various levels and end with the study of urban hierarchies (Rimmington, 1969, p. 9).

This gives us a hierarchy of generalizations, concepts and skills upon which to base an evaluation program.

So far, however, the notion of human development has not been considered; it must be considered now, for this is the other dimension, without consideration of which we could be guilty of expecting a particular behaviour form before maturation has made it possible. Human development is a very complex field, of which we are able only to scratch the surface in this context. All would tend to agree that every human being passes through a number of stages in physical, mental and moral development on the way to the achievement of maturity. Children vary in their rate of development, but the stages through which they pass are regarded as invariable and irreversible. Thus Piaget and his collaborators have discerned, through the accumulation of case studies, the existence of three main stages of cognitive development. Stage one, the period of sensori-motor intelligence, generally stretches from birth to the beginning of language development at about eighteen months. During this stage the child learns to repeat movements consciously. Stage two, which extends to about eleven or twelve years of age, consists of preparation for, and the achievement of, concrete operations in relation to classes, relations and numbers. Up till about four years there is a preconceptual sub-stage, followed by another sub-stage in which the child passes through an intuitive period. During this period there is difficulty in separating fantasy from reality, and an inability to engage in the logic of reversible thought. Children asked to construct a plan of the area where they live tend to do so only in terms of recollections of journeys actually made along particular streets, and are very subjective (Rhys, 1972). The important sub-stage from seven to eleven years is that in which the child begins to understand the relationship of landscape features to each other and to map symbols, and map distributions to realities, since he is now able to understand reversibility. The final stage, which tends to be completed by about the age of fourteen years, is the period of formal operations, during which the young adolescent learns to develop abstract thinking and higher levels of reasoning (Beard, 1969 and Sund, 1976). Those reaching this stage are able to analyze geographical areas they have never seen by the application of principles learned in concrete manner at the earlier stage. The principles are thus reinforced.

If Piaget is correct, it means that there are many young people in high schools at the concrete operational stage, most of whom will pass on to the formal operational stage before graduting. McNally's research (1974), however, has indicated that, at the Australian equivalent of the Grade VIII level, 77% of 112 students were still at the concrete operational stage, while at the grade X level 42,7% of 157 students had still not progressed beyond this level. Moreover, in the United States, McKinnon and Renner's research (Sund, 1976) has indicated that, far from all students having reached the formal operational stage by grade XII level, some 50% of a sample of 131 freshman students at Oklahoma City University operated completely at the concrete operational level. Only 25% had fully attained the ability to work wholly at the level of formal operations. There is no reason to think that Canadian high school students are substantially different We can assume only that the proportion of formal thinkers will increase, that concrete operational thinkers will decrease, and that many will be at a half-way stage between the two, as progression is made from grade VII to XII or XIII.

The question then arises as to whether, as a teacher, one should work wholly within this limitation or whether teaching and evaluation could themselves help to effect progress from one stage to another. Piaget notes that socially different environments retard or accelerate development through the stages, and that this differential "shows that stages are not purely a question of the maturation of the nervous system but are dependent upon interaction with the social environment and with experience in general" (Piaget, 1971, p. 7). There is, one may conclude, an obvious genetic limit to the speed with which a student may pass from one stage to another, but it has to be emphasized that we are not working within a rigidly determined time-frame. Abercrombie (Beard, 1969) has shown that freshmen students at the University of London who were not fully formally operational, in that they were unable to use scientific data to solve slightly unfamiliar problems, could be helped on to the attainment of this stage by sponsoring discussion among small groups relative to their experiments and observations. Presumably, evaluation that forms part of any particular curriculum could vary from stage to stage, helping students in attaining the next stage, as well as measuring whether or not a stage has been reached.

However, there are serious problems attached to any attempt to link evaluation with Piagetian stages. Despite all that has been said about Piaget's work, he is not without his detractors. R. M. Gagné, for instance, views the development of the intellect as "the building of increasingly complex and interacting structures of learned capabilities and the entities and skills which are learned, built upon each other in a cumulative fashion" (Ayers, 1971, p. 250). He refers, *inter alia*, to the process of acquiring a chain of concepts as "rule learning". Thus the tendency for the centres of large towns and cities to become areas where businesses predominate, where houses are being demolished, and where high-rise buildings are on the increase, involves the learning of a series of inter-linked concepts or "rules" (Graves, 1975, p. 173). Similarly, G. A. Ferguson suggests that "abilities emerge through a process of differential transfer and exert their effects differentially in learning situations" (Ayers, 1971, p. 250). Moreover F. A. Slater has also demonstrated, in her study of the relationship between Piaget's theory of intellectual development, Bruner's hypothesis, and levels of learning in geography, a statistically significant variation in the kind of geography learned from grade to grade, but one which does not appear to reflect Piaget's theory. (Slater, 1970). All agree fundamentally with each other in stressing the greater importance of learning in development, and disagree with the idea of biologically determined stages.

There are also other difficulties in trying to use Piagetian stages as the basis of a hierarchy of curriculum and evaluation entities. Lovell notes that, though one may reasonably conclude, admittedly on the basis of scattered and fragmentary evidence, that tasks involving formal operations have little transfer value for most students before thirteen years of age, we are not yet at the point where we can assert with even reasonable confidence the types of teaching and evaluation exercises that are most conducive to the development of formal operational thinking (Lovell, 1971). Even more disconcerting is the disparity between the development of formal operational thinking in the various subjects and even within subjects. The available data suggests that formal operations in historical geography appear much later than in physical geography. Moreover, as Piaget and his colleagues admit, neither adolescents nor adults operate all the time at the formal level. People work at different levels during the course of a day, according to their familiarity with and interest in subject matter with which they are faced (Lovell, 1971).

The question now is, should the teacher faced by the necessity for evaluating, attempt to use present knowledge of the Piagetian stages, or should he concentrate entirely on Bruner's spiral, or ignore both of them? Despite its problems, there is a good case for using Piaget's stages to some extent, for without some real concern for child development we should certainly, as was indicated earlier, be guilty of expecting too much or not enough of the student. One may visualize evaluation exercises in which questions may be answered either by concrete operational thinking or formal operational thinking. Thus the question: "What would happen to the coastline and shape of Nova Scotia if the sea level were lowered by one hundred feet?" requires only concrete operational thinking if the student is already well acquainted with the province. If, however, the supplement is added, "What other changes would occur?" it would give plenty of scope for formal operational thinking. Or the teacher may provide the opportunity for experiences that, for some students, may remain at the concrete level, but for others would provide the opportunities for advancement to the formal level. McNally records, when writing about one of his own social studies teaching units on Indonesia, that one girl was so excited by the appearance of an Indonesian shadow puppet, that three weeks later she presented, with other members of her group, a self-written play on *Indonesian Life*, using the shadow puppet. McNally sums up this experience by stating the child's

> "knowing" of this object was now much more 'operative', the evaluation in this case being detailed observation of the child's behaviour and recording of the advancement made (McNally, 1974, p. 128).

An important aspect of the work was to provide, in a relatively free environment, for behaviours that would show to a skilled observer clear evidence of advancement. Quite obviously, in order to do this, the teacher must himself have a clearly defined sense of the Piagetian stages, so that evaluation can relate to a progressive continuum.

The present writer does not, however, accept that it is possible to limit evaluation to conformity with Piagetian stages, for in learning geography (and the social sciences generally) the student is also appropriating culture forms. We need to be able to measure the degree of success with which a student has developed certain skills, concepts, generalizations and attitudes that are valued in the discipline of geography. Much, of course, depends upon one's view of evaluation. Whether one uses formal testing devices or relies upon observational techniques is a matter of personal preference. The present writer would tend to stress the use of skilled observation techniques, using check lists based upon the skills and concepts students might reasonably acquire at a particular grade level. This would include the assessment of presentations, both written and oral, which would tend to increase in importance as progress is made through the grades. Where teacher-made tests are used they should increase in sophistication with the years by requiring, not the recall of isolated facts, but thinking at varying and clearly defined levels (Logan and Rimmington, 1969, pp. 299-300).

In conclusion, one has to admit that insufficient research has so far been conducted in the longitudinal aspects of evaluation in geography. The Piagetian framework, as we have seen, has not yet been clearly related to school work, not enough anyway for us to be able to use it as anything more than a very rough guide for developing evaluation exercises. Moreover, as we have also noted, there is little agreement on curriculum, because of the nature of the discipline with which we are concerned. So that to speak of a graded scheme of evaluation in these circumstances is premature, rather like having a cart without a horse. All that one can really say at this stage is that logic demands the acceptance of differentiation, that there will be different expectations at different levels, and that much work needs to be done in developing evaluation systems that relate to particular curricula and the known facts of human development.

BIBLIOGRAPHY

Much of the material in this essay is taken from the author's "Evaluation in History and the Social Studies: The Longitudinal Aspect and Its Problems", *The History and Social Science Teacher*, 12 (iv) (Summer 1977).

AYERS, J. D., in GREEN, D. R., *et al.* (eds), *Measurement and Piaget* (New York: McGraw-Hill, 1971).

BEARD, R. M., *An Outline of Piaget's Developmental Psychology for Students and Teachers* (New York: Basic Books, 1969).

BRUNER, J. S., *The Process of Education* (Cambridge, Mass.: Harvard University Press, 1960).

GAGE, N. L., and BERLINER, D. C., *Educational Psychology* (Chicago: Rand McNally, 1975).

GRAVES, N. J., *Geography in Education* (London: Heinemann Educational Books Ltd., 1975).

LOGAN, L. M., and RIMMINGTON, G. T., *Social Studies: A Creative Direction* (Toronto: McGraw-Hill, 1969).

LOVELL, K., in GREEN, D. R., *et al.* (eds.). *Measurement and Piaget* (New York: McGraw-Hill, 1971).

McNALLY, D. W., *Piaget, Education and Teaching* (Lewes, England: New Educational Press, 1974).

PIAGET, J., in GREEN D. R., *et al.* (eds.), *Measurement and Piaget* (New York: McGraw-Hill, 1971).

RHYS, W., "The Development of Logical Thinking", in GRAVES, N. J. (ed.), *New Movements in the Study and Teaching of Geography* (London: Maurice Temple Smith, 1972).

RIMMINGTON, G. T., "Some Thoughts on Curriculum Development in Geography", *Manitoba Journal of Education* V (1) (November 1969).

SLATER, F. A., "The relationship between levels of learning in geography, Piaget's theory of intellectual development and Bruner's teaching 'hypothesis'", *Geographical Education*, 1 (ii) (1970).

SUND, R. B., *Piaget for Educators* (Columbus, Ohio: Charles E. Merrill, 1976).

THE TEACHER

L'ENSEIGNANT

FONDEMENTS THÉORIQUES DE LA GÉOGRAPHIE ET APPLICATIONS PÉDAGOGIQUES

Roch Choquette
Université de Sherbrooke

INTRODUCTION

Quelles sont les contributions intellectuelles de la géographie, lui justifiant une place de choix, dans les grilles-horaires du cours secondaire ? Voilà certes une question fondamentale et en même temps d'actualité, si on se réfère aux nombreuses modifications proposées qui influenceront à la fois, l'esprit et la séquence du cours de géographie pour l'enseignement secondaire. Cette ré-évaluation du cours secondaire est présentement un sujet d'actualité au Québec, mais la tendance déborde les cadres de cette province. Face à ces réaménagements, il faut éviter que la géographie et les sciences humaines soient reléguées à un second plan, faute d'avoir établi clairement leurs contributions intellectuelles à l'enseignement primaire et secondaire. Les universitaires au Québec ont toujours accepté l'apport important de la géographie au secteur des sciences de l'homme, mais très rares sont les oeuvres de vulgarisation pouvant contribuer à mettre en évidence l'apport intellectuel spécifique de l'enseignement de la géographie par des cheminements pédagogiques appropriés.

Trop souvent des conceptions fausses et partielles de l'enseignement de cette discipline, incitent les professeurs du secondaire à axer presqu'exclusivement leur enseignement sur la localisation, l'énumération et la description des éléments d'un espace géographique étudié. Localiser, décrire et énumérer ce que l'on observe est sûrement louable, mais on ne peut certes pas affirmer et prouver que les habiletés et les comportements intellectuels suscités par une telle démarche sont exclusifs à la géographie et correspondent aux spécificités de l'apport intellectuel de cette matière à l'enseignement secondaire.

Dans un premier temps, cet article se fixe comme objectif de mettre en évidence quelques concepts-clefs, justifiant l'unicité de la géographie au niveau de sa contribution intellectuelle à l'enseignement secondaire. Pour ce faire, nous procéderons à une analyse très sommaire des courants intellectuels ayant marqué les principaux jalons de l'évolution de cette discipline. Dans un deuxième temps, en se référant à quelques concepts polarisateurs de la géographie, nous tenterons d'élaborer un schéma de cheminement pédagogique conforme à ceux-ci. Dans une troisième étape, nous examinerons les conséquences de l'esprit d'un tel cheminement pédagogique face à la réorganisation des séquences du contenu d'un cours de géographie régionale, dans ce cas-ci, il s'agira du cours de Géographie du Canada, Géographie 470-412. Enfin, nous jugerons de la valeur relative de cette dernière approche en comparant celle-ci avec une démarche plus traditionnelle de l'étude d'un contenu de géographie régionale.

I. — LES PRINCIPAUX COURANTS DE LA PENSÉE GÉOGRAPHIQUE ET L'URGENCE D'UNE CONCEPTION PÉDAGOGIQUE RENOUVELÉE

Une vision très large de la géographie définit celle-ci comme étant l'étude de la différenciation spatiale de la terre. Cette définition classique visait surtout à mettre en évidence la description au détriment de l'explication. En s'inspirant de l'article de John M. Hunter[1], où il s'efforce de représenter sous la forme d'un tableau schématique, l'armature, l'esprit et les fonctions des diverses composantes de la géographie, Pierre Dagenais[2] a repris les modèles conceptuels de la géographie de Hagget, Fenneman, Hartshorne et enfin de Hunter lui-même, pour proposer sa propre conception de la géographie. Par cette étude, il a clairement mis en évidence et explicité schématiquement les fondements conceptuels spécifiques à la géographie. Des concepts-clefs comme la nature multidisciplinaire de la matière, la fonction carrefour de la géographie, les relations homme-milieu, etc. prennent une dimension concrète, nous permettant de saisir davantage le rôle de la géographie par rapport aux autres disciplines. Il existe cependant un dénominateur commun qui doit dominer les concepts précédents, si nous voulons comprendre les tendances contemporaines de la géographie.

> La géographie, pour s'élever à la dignité de science, s'efforce de passer de l'état qualitatif et descriptif à *l'état quantitatif* et *causal*. Elle prétend remonter aux causes : elle entend être *explicative*; toutes ses démarches : description, observation, comparaison, sont guidées par un concept qui de près ou de loin relève de la notion courante de causalité[3].

Ainsi de purement descriptive, la géographie contemporaine, même au niveau secondaire, devient plus explicative dans le cadre d'une recherche des facteurs physiques et humains pouvant nous permettre de comprendre le pourquoi d'un paysage géographique. Évidemment, le professeur du secondaire est peut-être conscient de ces nouvelles dimensions de la géographie contemporaine, mais vous

---

[1] J.M. Hunter, "The structure of Geography, Note on an introductary Model", *The Journal of Geography, vol. LXX, n° 6*, (1971), pp. 332, 336.

[2] Pierre Dagenais, « Cinq schémas théoriques de la géographie », Didactique-Géographie, vol. II, n° 7 (avril 1973), pp. 73, 79.

[3] René Clozier, *Histoire de la géographie*, P.U.F., Que sais-je, 1962, p. 116.

conviendrez qu'il existe dans bien des cas un écart important entre les concepts théoriques définissant la géographie et l'orientation pédagogique quotidienne. Il nous apparaît tout de même pressant de réduire ce fossé.

> La démarche de la pensée à laquelle il convient d'inviter les élèves n'*est autre que la recherche des liens entre les forces physiques et les forces vivantes* qui expliquent un paysage ou un trait de paysage, sur une partie localisée du globe[4].

Si nous refusons de réajuster l'orientation de notre enseignement dans le sens de démarches plus interrogatives et globalisantes, les propos de Debesse-Arvisset pourraient dans un avenir immédiat s'avérer prophétiques face à la place qu'occuperait la géographie dans les programmes d'enseignement secondaire.

> Par son objet, elle [la géographie] invite à de nouveaux rapports avec la nature, à un sentiment d'accord avec le milieu terrestre contraignant et beau, qui sollicite une action féconde disposant à y être heureux.
> *Si la géographie scolaire refuse ce point de vue, surgira une discipline qui sous le nom d'écologie*, ou d'environnement, ou autre vocable de naturologie, y pourvoira à sa place. Et si l'école ne veut pas, la jeunesse le découvrira : elle le fait déjà[5].

De ces constatations ressort l'objectif global des chapitres qui suivront : mettre en évidence une approche pédagogico-géographique centrée sur les concepts-clefs de la géographie orientés dans le sens d'un apprentissage où une perception globale et synthétique du milieu serait davantage favorisée.

II. — LE CONCEPT DE LIENS GÉOGRAPHIQUES ET D'ADÉQUATION PÉDAGOGIQUE

B. James et L. M. Crape[6] nous offrent une piste intéressante nous permettant d'amorcer une démarche pédagogique concrète mettant en évidence l'interdépendance des facteurs physiques et humains dans l'explication et la compréhension géographique de divers milieux. Les auteurs conçoivent trois types de liens ou de relations pouvant nous amener à concevoir un milieu géographique.

Le premier type de relations se réfère à *l'explication d'éléments du milieu naturel (N) ou physique* (sol, sous-sol, géomorphologie, végétation, etc.) par d'autres éléments physiques ou naturels (N).

En second lieu, les éléments de paysages géographiques résultant de l'action de l'homme, que les auteurs qualifient de facteurs ou d'éléments humains (H) peuvent être compris par d'autres facteurs

---

⁴ DEBESSE-ARVISSET, *L'environnement à l'école, une révolution pédagogique*, Collection S.V.P., 1973, p. 29.

⁵ *Ibid*, p. 134.

⁶ B. JAMES et L. M. CRAPE, *Geography for Today's Children*, New York, Appleton Century Crafts, 325 pages.

explicatifs de la même catégorie que ces derniers éléments humains (H).

Enfin un troisième type de relations recoupe les deux précédents en mettant l'emphase sur l'explication des facteurs humains (H) par des éléments du milieu naturel ou physique (N).

Pour mieux comprendre la démarche logique de cette approche, nous expliciterons au moyen d'exemples chacun des trois types de liens ou de relations géographiques que l'on peut développer avec des élèves du secondaire.

1. Les liens entre les facteurs naturels peuvent s'illustrer au moyen de l'exemple suivant :

Exemple : Le faible niveau des précipitations et les basses températures sont des éléments du milieu physique importants dans l'explication et la compréhension du type de végétation de conifères que l'on retrouve dans le moyen-nord canadien : référence aux isothermes et isolignes de la saison végétative. Donc végétation, facteur naturel (N), s'explique essentiellement par le climat, un autre facteur naturel (N).

On doit compléter ce lien de causalité simple en ajoutant d'autres éléments explicatifs tels que la pédologie, le relief, etc., nous permettant de mieux circonscrire l'ensemble des facteurs explicatifs pouvant nous permettre de comprendre le type de végétation selon l'exemple ci-haut mentionné. En plus, il faut remarquer que ces liens de causalité peuvent être réversibles : le climat influence grandement le type de végétation qu'on retrouve à un endroit donné, par contre certaines formes de végétation jouant un rôle d'écran pourront favoriser l'existence d'un micro-climat. Concrètement, en suivant cette démarche explicative, non seulement nous incitons l'étudiant à vouloir comprendre le pourquoi des phénomènes étudiés, mais aussi à concevoir à la fois la globalité et l'interdépendance des éléments qui composent le milieu naturel.

2. Les facteurs humains (H) considérés comme éléments explicatifs d'un paysage géographique résultant surtout de l'initiative de l'homme.

Exemple : Si nous prenons l'existence de cultures maraîchères que l'on retrouve autour de grandes villes, on peut dire que celles-ci s'expliquent surtout en fonction du marché des villes pour ces produits agricoles. Ainsi un paysage géographique résultant de l'initiative de l'homme comme la culture maraîchère s'explique essentiellement par un autre facteur humain (H) comme la demande du marché.

Évidemment pour mettre en évidence les principaux types de liens géographiques, nos exemples sont réduits à leur plus simple expression. Il est évident que d'autres facteurs humains d'ordre économique peuvent expliquer ce type de culture maraîchère en plus des facteurs physiques tels que le sol, le climat, le relief, etc. qui complètent l'inventaire des phénomènes explicatifs de notre paysage humanisé. L'insistance sur les éléments du milieu physique comme explicatifs d'un élément humain nous amène à mettre en évidence un troisième type de lien géographique.

3. Une dernière perception des liens géographiques envisage l'explication de facteurs humains en fonction surtout des éléments du cadre naturel :

Exemple : La concentration des forêts de conifères du Québec et l'orientation du réseau hydrographique sont des facteurs physiques importants pouvant expliquer globalement la localisation des usines de pâtes et papiers le long des aflluents du Saint-Laurent. Cet exemple met clairement en évidence comment les éléments du milieu naturel expliquent et orientent des facteurs humains du paysage géographique telle l'existence d'usines de pâtes et papiers. Cependant, ce genre de lien géographique ne doit jamais être poussé à outrance comme causes explicatives, car il existe toujours des causes humaines de types historique, économique ou culturel nous permettant une saisie plus globale et réaliste.

En résumé selon les exemples précédents, nous constatons que les principaux liens géographiques peuvent se ramener aux trois affirmations suivantes :

1. Le (N) facteur naturel s'explique par d'autres facteurs naturels (N).

2. Le (H) facteur humain s'explique par d'autres facteurs humains (H).

3. Le (H) facteur humain s'explique par d'autres facteurs naturels (N).

Nous avons cependant constaté que les facteurs explicatifs sont rarement uniques, ainsi nous pouvons synthétiser ces approches au moyens des deux schémas suivants :

1. Un facteur naturel (N) s'explique par :

Facteurs naturels 1 — _____

2 — _____

3 — _____

4 — _____

2. Un facteur humain (H) s'explique par :

Facteurs (N)	Facteurs (H)
1 — _____	1 — _____
2 — _____	2 — _____
3 — _____	3 — _____
4 — _____	4 — _____

Sommairement, cette approche pédagogique axée sur les liens géographiques, concrétise une façon de penser où le professeur met en évidence le relationnel, l'interdépendance des phénomènes étudiés. Cette présentation d'un contenu géographique abandonne le plan tiroir au profit d'une approche globale plus fidèle à l'idée de la géographie comme discipline-synthèse et plus conforme au concept d'écosystème. Il nous apparaît évident que la géographie aura un rôle primordial sur le plan éducatif dans la mesure où elle pourra par sa démarche pédagogique mettre en évidence la notion d'écosystème, conciliable avec les qualificatifs de discipline-carrefour et de science-synthèse qu'on lui attribue.

III. — DE LA THÉORIE DES LIENS GÉOGRAPHIQUES À L'APPLICATION PÉDAGOGIQUE

Ayant consacré le chapitre précédent à examiner les combinaisons possibles pouvant nous permettre une compréhension schématique des différentes formes que peuvent prendre les explications géographiques, cette partie du document proposera quelques exemples de cheminements pédagogiques.

Prenons comme exemple le cas où le professeur doit enseigner un cours portant sur la Mauricie. Après examen du contenu, il décide d'aborder cette étude par la formulation de questions pertinentes sur les phénomènes particuliers de cette région, comme par exemple les raisons de l'établissement des usines de pâtes et papiers dans la Mauricie. Schématiquement son travail de préparation pourra s'élaborer de la façon suivante.

Le pourquoi de l'établissement des usines de pâtes et papiers dans la Mauricie ?

Facteurs (N) naturels   Facteurs (H) humains

— _____   — _____

— _____   — _____

— _____   — _____

                                    — _____

Dans une seconde étape, son travail consistera à découvrir les facteurs explicatifs pouvant l'éclairer sur l'interrogation première. Au moyen d'une documentation variée (cartes, volumes, graphiques, annuaires, statistiques, etc.), il formulera les facteurs susceptibles d'expliquer le pourquoi de son affirmation première. Ces explications seront regroupées sous les titres de facteurs (N) naturels et (H) humains telles qu'indiquées dans le schéma. Évidemment selon le niveau d'enseignement, les explications fournies pour l'élaboration des facteurs (N) naturels et (H) humains seront adaptées aux capacités intellectuelles spécifiques à chaque niveau du secondaire. Pour concrétiser ces explications, des moyens de représentation appropriés (cartes, diagrammes, photos, statistiques, etc.), mettront mieux en lumière les facteurs explicatifs.

L'étape finale de la préparation d'un cours à partir de l'exemple mentionné pourra prendre la forme schématique suivante. L'établissement des usines de pâtes et papiers de la Mauricie s'explique par :

Facteurs (N)

1 — Rivière Saint-Maurice (transport du bois et énergie hydro-électrique);
2 — Forêt abondante de conifères (matière première);

3 — Fleuve Saint-Laurent (route naturelle favorisant les exportations).

Facteurs (H)

1 — Main d'oeuvre disponible;

2 — Décisions gouvernementales et politiques (octrois, droits de coupe de bois);
3 — Marché important (demande pour le papier au Canada et aux États-Unis);
4 — Réseaux de transport routier et ferroviaire..

Une fois les facteurs mentionnés, le professeur amènera les étudiants à réfléchir sur les éléments explicatifs les plus polarisateurs. Par exemple, les éléments comme la matière première (bois), la rivière Saint-Maurice et la demande importante pour le papier peuvent être considérés comme des facteurs déterminants par rapport à l'ensemble des causes explicatives.

Enfin une troisième étape dans notre démarche pourra consister à mettre l'emphase sur les *conséquences* d'un tel développement industriel. Ainsi il y a l'exploitation de cette ressource naturelle et la forme que pourra prendre le reboisement. Dans le même sens, il y a aussi la dimension pollution du milieu qu'entraîne une telle exploitation. Il y a des conséquences plus positives comme le développement économique réalisé grâce à une telle exploitation et les perspectives d'avenir.

La valeur d'une telle préparation se veut surtout axée sur la qualité de la réflexion personnelle du professeur, en plus des sources diversifiées de documentation dont il peut disposer. Il n'est alors plus question de devancer les étudiants en résumant et schématisant le contenu des chapitres à voir. Au contraire, la qualité de la réflexion personnelle par rapport aux thèmes et l'adaptation de la matière aux divers niveaux académiques deviennent des critères essentiels de cette démarche. Évidemment, les premières tentatives exigeront un effort de réflexion plus intense que celui exigé lors de l'acquisition mécanique du savoir. Mais tout compte fait, il apparaît avantageux d'oeuvrer dans cette perspective de l'utilisation du savoir géographique exploitant davantage une démarche intellectuelle spécifique à la géographie.

L'exemple précédent a mis en évidence l'approche en fonction d'une échelle régionale, mais la démarche pourrait s'appliquer à d'autres niveaux comme à ceux d'une ville, d'un quartier ou d'une province. Ainsi les questions d'amorce pourraient être les suivantes si on étudie un phénomène local : les facteurs justifiant l'établissement des principales industries de notre ville ou le pourquoi de la localisation des centres commerciaux de notre ville. À une autre échelle, on pourrait amorcer l'étude d'une région plus vaste en s'interrogeant sur les facteurs physiques et humains favorisant l'axe industriel Québec-Windsor ou sur les facteurs justifiant la production de blé dans les provinces de l'ouest.

IV. — L'AGENCEMENT DES CURRICULUMS ET UNE CONNAISSANCE GLOBALE DES ÉLÉMENTS DES MILIEUX GÉOGRAPHIQUES

Au Québec la conception de la géographie, que l'on retrouve aujourd'hui dans les programmes de géographie régionale du secondaire, reflète une approche s'inspirant grandement de l'école Française voire même européenne de la première moitié du XXe siècle. Si on prend par exemple le cours de Géographie du Canada Géographie 412 (voir Annexe 1), on constate cette tendance analytique à aborder d'abord des éléments de géographie physique et humaine pour ensuite procéder à des études régionales.

De cette démarche suggérée par le M.E.Q. et utilisée par la très grande majorité des professeurs du secondaire, on constate plusieurs lacunes faussant selon nous, l'essentiel de la conception de notre discipline. En premier lieu, une telle structure du contenu favorise d'abord presque uniquement l'acquisition de connaissances et très peu la compréhension des éléments géographiques explicatifs d'un paysage géographique. De plus, selon certains professeurs, les étudiants perdaient dès le début, le goût de l'étude de cette discipline. Comment s'en étonner quand on songe qu'on leur imposait des notions aussi abstraites que la structure morphologique et les sortes de roches rencontrées au Canada, sans aucun lien avec les éléments humains auxquels se rattachent ces facteurs physiques. On donne parfois l'impression de faire des sciences de la terre pendant une partie de l'année, et des sciences de l'homme pendant l'autre.

Dans la préface de son dernier ouvrage, Peter Haggett insiste sur cette fausse optique que l'on peut donner à la géographie, en agençant artificiellement les éléments physiques et humains d'un curriculum.

> Lying athwart both the physical and social sciences, geography challenges students to abandon familiar and comfortable "straight jackets" and to focus directly on *relationships* between man and his environnement, their spacial consequences and the resulting regional structures that have emerged on the earth surface...
> ... It is all to easy to take the view that all one can or should do is to have a student take introductory courses in various easily identifiable subfields physical geography, cultural geography, and so on and hope that somehow these will produce an integrated view of geography as a whole. The

osmosis, however, by which this is supposed to take place is rarely clearly defined[7].

D'autre part, les auteurs d'un manuel scolaire anglophone *Canada this land of ours* ont bien saisi cette problématique dans l'élaboration de leur ouvrage.

> Canada this land of ours divides Canada into seven geographic regions with cut across provincial boundaries. Each region has been written with what the authors call *an organic approach*. There is no formula of climate, vegetation, soil and so forth repeated in regular order, chapter after chapter, instead topics are introduced where they have validity. For exemple, the climate of the St-Laurence Lowland is related to the Quebec Winter Carnival and the formation of sedementary rock to petroleum exploration in the Prairies[8].

En s'inspirant de cette même idée fondamentale axée sur une compréhension géographique en fonction des relations existant entre l'homme et son milieu physique, nous avons de même produit un curriculum (voir Annexe 2), portant sur le même contenu que le cours Géographie 412, mais en insistant davantage sur le rationnel. Par cette nouvelle orientation du contenu, nous voulons surtout intégrer les faits physiques à l'explication de thèmes essentiellement humains (agriculture, pêche, industrialisation, etc.) lorsque ceux-ci deviennent des facteurs explicatifs. Nous supposons que l'étudiant pourrait ainsi plus facilement saisir l'influence du physique sur l'homme et vice-versa. Pour concrétiser l'optique de notre curriculum, nous avons prévu des exercices d'apprentissage appropriés visant à développer d'une manière séquentielle les concepts et habiletés. Grâce à un travail de collaboration, nous avons produit un document d'environ deux cent soixante-quinze (275) pages de notes, d'exercices et d'activités pédagogiques variés : lecture de photos, de cartes, interprétation de graphiques, jeux de simulation etc. Les dernières retouches et des ajouts importants au document ont été effectués par monsieur Réjean Rousseau, professeur de géographie à la Polyvalente de Thetford-Mines.

V. — DE LA THÉORIE À L'EXPÉRIMENTATION

Les professeurs du secondaire semblaient favorables en principe à cette approche pédagogique et à l'agencement du contenu d'un curriculum favorisant le concept de liens géographiques par une intégration des facteurs humains et physiques à l'intérieur d'un même thème d'étude.

Par contre ce même milieu manifestait certaines réticences face à l'application concrète de cette approche. Les réserves touchaient surtout les aspects suivants :

---

[7] Peter HAGGET, *Geography a Modern Synthesis*, Harper and Row, 1975, p. XII (préface).

[8] EN COLLABORATION, *Canada : This Land of Ours*, 1977, p. 1.

1. Le programme de géographie régionale du Canada (Géographie 470-412) ne permet pas un tel écart dans l'agencement du curriculum pour appliquer l'approche proposée.

2. Les examens de fin d'année évaluent le contenu du curriculum tel qu'élaboré par le ministère, et par conséquent un nouvel agencement de celui-ci désavantagerait les étudiants face aux examens officiels du ministère.

3. Les élèves du secondaire III ou IV ne sont pas encore parvenus à un degré de développement intellectuel et n'ont pas la maturité nécessaire pour fonctionner selon cette logique.

À ces réticences, nous opposions les arguments suivants :

1. Le programme actuel (Géographie 470-412) peut nous permettre des réaménagements favorisant un enseignement plus systématique des liens géographiques en se référant à l'énoncé suivant qu'on retrouve en préliminaire du plan d'étude.

> L'étude des tendances de l'économie des principaux secteurs canadiens devrait leur montrer une vue d'ensemble de la géographie du Canada, tout en leur permettant *d'établir les relations nécessaires* entre les facteurs physiques, humains et économiques...
> ... Enfin l'acquisition des données de base semble plus importante que l'accumulation d'une foule de connaissances disparates. En plus d'être plus logique et plus formatrice, cette étude nous paraît plus intéressante que le traditionnel plan tiroir.

Pour nous, un tel énoncé de principe justifie l'approche que nous proposons, car notre objectif premier est justement d'expérimenter un cheminement, permettant à l'étudiant d'établir des relations entre les facteurs physiques et humains pour l'amener à une compréhension plus logique de la géographie.

2. Il nous semble évident que si les étudiants sont amenés à penser en terme de relationnel avec l'approche que nous proposons, ceux-ci au contraire devront être davantage préparés pour répondre au questionnaire de fin d'année du M.E.Q. En effet, car nous supposons qu'une connaissance logique de la matière implique aussi une connaissance du contenu.

3. Enfin, concernant le degré de développement intellectuel des étudiants à ce niveau du secondaire face aux exigences de l'approche proposée, nous croyons qu'à l'expérimentation, le taux de réussite nous donnerait raison.

Pour éclairer le débat, nous avons expérimenté durant une année scolaire notre approche auprès de trois classes, comprenant quatre-vingt-un étudiants choisis au hasard. Pour comparer, les services d'orientation de la Polyvalente de Thetford-Mines nous ont aidés à sélectionner trois autres classes-témoins, comparables à nos quatre-vingt-un étudiants du groupe expérimental au niveau du rendement scolaire moyen. Le seul exercice commun aux deux groupes était l'examen de fin d'année préparé par le ministère de l'Édution. Ce dernier examen devait nous permettre de comparer la qualité de l'apprentissage géographique pour les deux groupes. Pour faire cette comparaison, nous avons obtenu du ministère de l'Éducation l'autorisation de procéder à notre propre correction de l'examen final de juin afin de mettre en parallèle les résultats bruts non convertis. Ensuite, pour fin de comparaison, nous avons procédé à une classification taxonomique selon Bloom de chacune des questions de l'examen de juin 1978 pour le cours de Géographie 470-412.

Ces étapes franchies, voici l'hypothèse que nous pouvions vérifier :

> Pour les questions de niveaux taxonomiques « connaissance » les deux (2) groupes, expérimental et témoin, devraient avoir des résultats bruts équivalents alors que pour les questions de niveaux taxonomiques supérieurs, les étudiants du groupe expérimental devraient avoir des résultats bruts supérieurs à ceux du groupe-témoin.

La recherche fut dirigée par monsieur Réjean Rousseau qui s'est également occupé de la compilation des résultats. Un rapport final a été soumis au ministère de l'Éducation du Québec sous le titre : Géographie 470-412. Une approche systématique, projet 77-35. Nous nous permettons ici de tirer les grandes lignes des résultats à partir des tableaux-synthèses qu'on retrouve en Annexe 3.

D'abord sur les cinquante (50) questions de l'examen, quarante-six (46) furent retenues; les questions sept (7), onze (11), quatorze (14) et vingt (20) furent jugées inadéquates pour fin d'évaluation par les autorités du M.E.Q.

La distribution des questions selon les niveaux taxonomiques, nous a donné trente-trois (33) questions du niveau connnaissance correspondant au chiffre 1 du tableau, neuf (9) questions seulement pour le niveau application correspondant au chiffre 3 et enfin trois (3) questions d'analyse associées au chiffre 4.

Pour les questions du type connaissance (33 questions) les étudiants du groupe expérimental ont obtenu un taux de réussite supérieur à celui du groupe-témoin. 58% de réussite par rapport à 49% pour le groupe-témoin. Il en est de même pour les questions de compréhension, le groupe expérimental manifeste sa supériorité par 67,4% de réussite par rapport à 61,7% de réussite pour le groupe expérimental. Pour l'unique question mesurant l'application (question 49) les étudiants du groupe expérimental ont encore une fois eu un meilleur résultat : 37% de réussite contre 29,2% pour le groupe-témoin. Enfin, pour le quatrième niveau taxonomique le groupe expérimental est de nouveau supérieur 39,9% contre 32,2%. Ainsi, le groupe expérimental a partout des taux de réussite supérieurs au groupe-témoin, confirmant largement notre hypothèse de base. En plus, si nous comparons les notes finales du M.E.Q. des deux groupes en fonction des taux d'échec, le groupe-témoin qui comptait quatre-vingt-neuf (89) étudiants a vu onze (11) de ceux-ci échouer, soit un taux de 12%. Le groupe expérimental qui lui, comptait quatre-vingt-un (81) étudiants n'a eu que deux échecs soit un taux de 2,4%. Sur ce dernier point, considérant que les deux groupes étaient théoriquement comparables au niveau de leur potentiel intellectuel, ce qui fut vérifié au début de notre recherche, nous pouvons avec toute réserve déduire que l'approche utilisée est aussi bonne pour les étudiants dits allégés que pour les mieux pourvus.

Bref, à l'analyse des résultats notre hypothèse s'avère vérifiée, même que les étudiants du groupe expérimental ont réussi à avoir des résultats supérieurs pour les questions du niveau connaissance. Nous devons cependant à la lumière de cette expérimentation garder à l'esprit certaines réserves avant de conclure que la nouvelle approche proposée s'avère supérieure en tous points à l'approche proposée par le document du ministère. En effet, il y a les dimensions qualité des relations interpersonnelles que les professeurs peuvent avoir eues avec les étudiants et l'aspect de la valeur relative des activités d'apprentissage utilisées dans les deux cas. Donc globalement, en gardant en mémoire les réserves ci-haut mentionnées, notre approche s'est avérée plus valable que l'approche du ministère à la lumière des résultats obtenus aux examens du M.E.Q. de l'année scolaire 1977-78.

CONCLUSION

À notre époque, il est fondamental que l'enseignement de la géographie au niveau secondaire, s'oriente vers des apprentissages donnant à l'étudiant une vision globale des milieux étudiés. Concrètement, cela veut dire mettre davantage l'accent sur l'apprentissage des interrelations entre les phénomènes physiques et humains des espaces géographiques étudiés, véhiculant ainsi une perception plus juste des réalités selon une optique d'écosystème. Nous avons dans ce texte, proposé des démarches pédagogiques nous permettant de concrétiser ces concepts théoriques, en plus nous avons soumis à l'expérimentation, l'agencement d'un curriculum complet (GEO. 412) où les activités d'apprentissage sous-jacentes aux thèmes d'étude étaient axées davantage sur une compréhension des liens géographiques.

En bref, notre expérimentation nous a permis de conclure que les activités d'apprentissage de l'approche expérimentée ont permis aux étudiants d'un groupe expérimental, d'obtenir des résultats supérieurs à l'examen final du M.E.Q. pour juin 1978.

ANNEXE 1

1. *Le milieu physique :*

    A. Structure, morphologie, régions naturelles   12 périodes*
    B. Les climats   18   "

---

    * Le nombre de périodes est seulement indicatif; il faut respecter la proportion plutôt que la durée.

2. *Les activités de l'homme :*

A. La population	12 périodes	
B. Les activités primaires	28	"
C. Les activités secondaires	16	"
D. Les activités tertiaires	8	"
E. L'énergie	16	"

3. *Le Québec :*

A. L'agriculture	10 périodes	
B. L'industrie et le réseau urbain	16	"
C. La région montréalaise	8	"
D. Problèmes économiques du Québec	6	"

ANNEXE 2

GÉOGRAPHIE—412

APPROCHE SYSTÉMATIQUE

Introduction à l'Étude du Canada

— Introduction à la carte du Canada
  — La grille d'une carte
— Rose des vents
— Notion d'échelle
  — Échelle numérique
  — Échelle graphique
— Voyage au Canada

Dossier 1 : *La répartition de la population canadienne*

— Découverte de l'espace habité
  — Densité de population
  — Facteurs de localisation
— À la recherche des facteurs naturels de répartition de la population
  — Facteurs climatologiques
  — Minima et maxima
  — Moyennes thermiques
  — Écart thermique
  — Représentation cartographique des températures
  — Zones climatiques du Canada
— Facteurs morphologiques (reliefs)
  — Régions naturelles du Canada
— Première étape de développement.
— À la recherche des facteurs humains de répartition de la population
  — Historique du peuplement du Canada
  — Groupes ethniques
  — Deuxième étape de développement
— Étude de la population canadienne
  — L'accroissement de la population
  — Composantes démographiques
  — Accroissement naturel
  — Notion de taux

— Bilan migratoire
— Accroissement réel
— Structure de la population
   — Pyramide des âges
— Répartition de la population
   — Interdépendance des facteurs dans la répartition de la population

Dossier 2 :   *L'agriculture au Canada*

— Introduction
   — Le domaine agricole
   — La population agricole
— Recherche des facteurs
   — Le relief
   — Le climat
      • la température
      • les précipitations
      • le diagramme climatique
      • les zones climatiques
   — Les sols
   — Les noyaux agricoles
   — Types de cultures — définitions
   — La production agricole des différentes régions
   — La culture du blé
      • La Commission Canadienne du Blé
   — Élevage dans l'Ouest
   — Élevage laitier
   — Culture spécialisée
      • la culture fruitière
      • la culture du tabac
      • la culture de la pomme de terre
   — Éléments du paysage rural canadien
      • le rang
      • le township

Dossier 3 :   *Les richesses forestières et l'industrie du bois*

— Introduction
— Découvertes de l'espace forestier
— Recherche des facteurs naturels
— Exploitation des facteurs **naturels**
— Exploitation des ressources forestières
   — Les industries de transformation du bois
   — Valeur de la production forestière
   — Exportations forestières

Dossier 4 :   *Les ressources minières*

— Introduction
— L'origine des minéraux
— Les types de roches
   — Présentation
   — Les roches ignées
   — Les roches sédimentaires
   — Les roches métamorphiques
   — Le cycle de la roche
   — Formation des types de roches
   — Processus géomorphologiques
   — Agents d'érosion

— La formation du relief canadien
  — Le Bouclier canadien
  — La mer du Dévonien
  — Les Appalaches et les montagnes Innuitiennes
  — La mer du crétacée
  — Les Cordillières de l'Ouest
— Trois familles de minéraux
  — Minéraux métalliques ou métaux
  — Minéraux non-métalliques
  — Combustibles possibles
— Répartition des minéraux
— Les mines et le peuplement
— La production minérale du Canada
  — Valeur de production des grands minéraux
  — Production minérale par province
— Exportations minérales par province
— L'amiante
  — Distribution de l'amiante québécoise en 1972
  — Emplois et transformation

Dossier 5 : *Les pêches canadiennes*

— Facteurs de localisation des zones de pêche
  — Les zones d'eau profonde ou la plate-forme continentale
  — Les courants marins
— Localisation des zones de pêche
  — Les zones de l'Atlantique et du Pacifique
  — La zone des eaux intérieures
— Étude comparée de la production des deux principales zones de pêche

Dossier 6 : *L'Énergie*

— Présentation de l'hydrographie du Canada
— Quelques définitions en hydrologie
— Un réseau hydrographique très développé
  — Bassin de l'Atlantique
  — Bassin de la Baie d'Hudson
  — Bassin de l'Arctique
  — Bassin du Pacifique
  — Hydrographie du Québec
— La centrale hydro-électrique
— La centrale thermique conventionnelle
— La centrale thermo-nucléaire
— Qualités de l'énergie électrique
— Localisation des principales centrales électriques
— Production électrique canadienne
— Développement hydro-électrique de la Baie James
— Autres sources d'énergie
  — Pétrole et gaz naturel
    • Formation
    • Extraction
    • Les réserves canadiennes
    • Transport
    • Raffinage
  — La houille
    • Formation
    • Utilisation du charbon
— Consommation énergétique canadienne

Dossier 7 : *L'industrialisation*

— Potentiel industriel naturel canadien
  — Industrie primaire
  — Industrie secondaire
  — Secteurs d'activité primaire, secondaire et tertiaire
  — Potentiel industriel naturel des grandes régions du Canada
— Les facteurs de localisation industrielle
  — Le marché
  — La main d'oeuvre
  — La présence d'énergie
  — Les moyens de transport
  — Autres facteurs
— Localisation d'une aluminerie
  — Facteur prédominant
  — Les alumineries canadiennes
— Localisation d'une sidérurgie
  — Facteurs prédominants
  — Les aciéries canadiennes
— L'industrie automobile
— Localisation des industries-Synthèse
  — Facteurs de localisation des grandes industries
— Importance de l'industrie de transport au Canada
  — Structure de la population active
  — Les grandes zones industrielles du Canada
  — Grandes villes canadiennes
— Valeur de la production industrielle

Dossier 8 : *Le Québec*

— Vue d'ensemble des noyaux urbains
  — Population des zones urbaines
  — Les villes et leur cours d'eau
— Le Québec régional
  — Régions naturelles
  — Zones climatiques
  — Végétation naturelle
  — Régions minières
  — Site des villes
  — Régions administratives
  — Caractéristiques économiques des régions administratives.

ANNEXE 3

RÉSULTATS COMPARATIFS DE QUESTIONS

Numéros	1	2	3	4	5	6	8	9
Niveaux taxonomiques	1	1	2	1	1	2	1	1
% réussite Gr. Expérimental	35	66	69	19	84	26	85	60
% réussite Gr.-Témoin	58	58	57	18	46	26	69	71

10	12	13	15	16	17	18	19	21	22	23	24	25
1	1	2	1	1	1	2	1	4	4	1	1	1
80	35	75	88	75	67	75	66	57	16	49	71	56
69	27	80	74	72	73	46	67	30	09	45	55	49

26	27	28	29	30	31	32	33	34	35	36	37	38
1	1	1	4	1	1	1	1	1	1	1	1	2
29	86	65	46	65	44	31	16	40	61	66	45	96
29	31	55	57	54	30	30	15	31	62	48	45	84

39	40	41	42	43	44	45	46	47	48	49	50
1	1	1	1	1	1	2	2	2	2	3	1
56	81	71	67	51	60	77	57	55	49	38	94
47	25	57	78	56	48	76	58	51	46	29	93

%	Connaissance		Compréhension		Application		Analyse	
	S	%	S	%	S	%	S	
Gr. expérimental	58,372	2,045	67,407	1,755	37,037	5,399	39,918	3,010
Gr.-témoin	49,228	1,894	61,798	1,908	29,213	4,848	32,210	2,791

RÉFLEXIONS SUR L'ENSEIGNEMENT DE LA GÉOGRAPHIE URBAINE AU SECONDAIRE

MARCIEN VILLEMURE
Faculté d'Éducation
Université d'Ottawa.

Le présent article n'ambitionne pas de donner le contenu intégral d'une géographie urbaine au secondaire ou d'expliciter dans le moindre détail une méthode d'enseignement, ou encore de couvrir in extenso un aspect quelconque de cette géographie. Le sujet est trop vaste, trop fondamental pour le but que se fixe cet article. Tout au plus, ces réflexions voudront toucher à quelques points de cet enseignement, points que nous croyons importants et qui nous sont inspirés par notre expérience, certaines méthodes d'enseignement appropriées à cette matière ou encore par le contenu du programme-cadre du ministère de l'Éducation de l'Ontario, "Urban Studies", destiné aux élèves de secondaire IV (12e année de scolarité)[1].

Il est un fait que nous observons journellement chez nos étudiants, chez les élèves du secondaire et même chez ceux de l'élémentaire. Lorsque le professeur donne un « projet » de recherche, la première démarche que fait l'étudiant ou l'élève, avant même de réfléchir au sujet, c'est de se rendre à la bibliothèque pour y chercher des renseignements sur le sujet choisi ou, si celui-ci n'est pas encore identifié, pour dénicher parmi les volumes existants un sujet pour lequel il serait assuré de trouver une bonne documentation. C'est, pensons-nous, un mouvement naturel qui survient trop tôt et nous n'avons jamais raté l'occasion de le souligner. Il faut que, en plus de trouver un sujet, les élèves puissent y définir quelques grandes idées à développer et noter sur fiches les connaissances qu'ils possèdent déjà sur le sujet; tout cela avant de se rendre au centre de documentation. Cette habitude de recourir à eux-mêmes, à leurs connaissances, peut s'avérer d'une grande utilité. Il peut arriver, en stage d'enseignement, pour une raison ou une autre, qu'on demande à un étudiant-maître d'enseigner un point particulier à une heure d'avis. Cette habitude couperait court à la panique si l'étudiant-maître s'assoyait et calmement jetait sur papier les connaissances qu'il possède. Pour l'élève du secondaire et même celui de l'élémentaire, cette façon de procéder

_____
[1] PROVINCE D'ONTARIO, Ministère de l'Éducation, *Urban Studies*, Toronto, 1971.

serait bénéfique puisqu'il engagerait ses recherches avec beaucoup plus d'assurance, se rendant déjà compte qu'il ne part pas de zéro et qu'il produira un travail plus personnel. Le professeur pourra même par des questions judicieuses aider les élèves, spécialement ceux ce l'élementaire, à extérioriser leurs connaissances.

Si cette étape s'avère fructueuse pour un « projet » de recherche, pourquoi ne le serait-elle pas pour un cours, particulièrement au cycle sénior du secondaire, au sujet duquel les élèves possèdent déjà une connaissance empirique. C'est le cas, il nous semble, pour la géographie urbaine. Par l'intermédiaire de leur travail d'été ou du soir, de leurs loisirs, de leurs déplacements, de leurs achats, de leurs échanges en famille, avec leurs amis, avec leurs compagnons de travail, par l'intermédiaire de leurs observations, de leurs réflexions, les élèves possèdent sans contredit une connaissance empirique de la ville : ils ont « expérimenté » la ville par leurs différentes activités. C'est du vécu, du connu, de l'intégré. Bien entendu, ces connaissances sont diffuses, enchevêtrées, conscientes jusqu'à un certain point. Cependant, si le professeur leur donne l'occasion de mettre en lumière leurs connaissances, de les décortiquer, d'en faire l'inventaire, de les classer, il pose un acte des plus formateurs parce qu'il se situe dans la ligne d'une pédagogie qui développera chez eux une motivation et une confiance en soi. Nous irons plus loin en disant qu'il est tout indiqué que le professeur procède ainsi, s'il veut poser un acte significatif d'éducation.

Cette extériorisation des connaissances fera poindre les préjugés plus ou moins conscients de l'élève. Qu'il habite un quartier défavorisé, ou une banlieue résidentielle, l'élève n'aura pas la même perception de la ville : dans un cas comme dans l'autre il voit sa ville à travers des filtres qui ne sont rien d'autres que les préjugés véhiculés par son milieu socio-économique. Or, ne peut-on pas espérer qu'un cours de géographie urbaine puisse effacer un tant soit peu ces préjugés ? Ne peut-on pas espérer que l'emploi de la méthode scientifique puisse contribuer à donner une façon de penser qui ne permette pas aux préjugés de prendre racine ? La ville est un objet d'étude et la méthode utilisée doit permettre l'objectivité. De plus, le développement de l'attitude scientifique pourra, par transfert, élargir les horizons nationalistes ou provincialistes.

De toute évidence, en agissant ainsi, le professeur pourra mieux donner un goût profond des études urbaines, arriver à former des citoyens intéressés, engagés. Et les raisons ne manquent pas pour le convaincre de la nécessité de tels objectifs. On peut déjà prévoir qu'au Canada, en l'an 2 000, 80% de la population vivra dans les villes, dont la majorité dans de grandes villes. Ce fait ne nous invite certainement pas à sous-estimer le rôle des études urbaines au secondaire. Comme la géographie nationale, mais non au même titre, elles doivent avoir une place de choix. Les villes sont le coeur de nos sociétés, elles y jouent un rôle des plus significatifs elles en sont les bougies d'allumage. La traditionnelle classification en milieux urbain et rural s'estompe pour faire place aux environs des grandes villes à ce qu'il est convenu d'appeler le champs urbain. (Ce cours peut s'adresser à tout étudiant, qu'il habite une grande, moyenne ou petite ville ou la campagne, puisque la grande ville est omniprésente.)

En plus d'être un lieu de travail et de résidence, de services de toutes sortes, la ville est un « milieu d'évolution, de transformation, de formation, d'information, de concentration cérébrale et financière, d'invention, de progrès technique, de promotion individuelle[2] ». Il y a donc lieu d'enseigner la géographie urbaine avec le plus de vision, d'humanisme, et de méthode possible. Il y a donc lieu d'amener l'élève à réaliser que ce milieu sera le sien pour plusieurs années à venir, qu'il le recevra en héritage et que, par conséquent, il doit aujourd'hui s'y intéresser, être alerte et vigilant à son égard. D'autant plus que tout laisse prévoir que son niveau de vie ne sera pas aussi élevé que celui d'après-guerre et que même celui d'aujourd'hui. Autrement dit, d'une part, il aura moins de moyens d'éviter ce qui pour nous sont des inconvénients de la ville et d'autre part, il doit en retour déjà s'intéresser à la qualité de la vie urbaine de sorte qu'il puisse jouir avec le plus d'intensité possible de son droit de cité.

De plus, connaître le milieu urbain implique que l'élève puisse comprendre que chaque ville est un maillon d'une chaîne, qu'il puisse réaliser, causes à l'appui, l'ampleur de la croissance mondiale. Même si au contraire, il est préférable que les études portent surtout sur les villes nord-américaines, il est tout de même essentiel que l'élève ait une connaissance des villes d'autres continents, spécialement celles des pays sous-développés.

Ouvrons une parenthèse sur les objectifs décrits jusqu'à présent pour répondre à une question que se pose sûrement le practicien. « Former des citoyens pour l'an 2 000 », « apprendre à l'étudiant à domestiquer sa ville », « montrer le rôle de bougie d'allumage de la ville », « donner le goût des études urbaines » : avons-nous là des voeux pieux, des objectifs, des buts ? Pourtant nous rencontrons souvent de telles expressions dans les programmes d'étude, les plans de cours, etc. Graves[3] nous permet de faire la lumière sur cette question. Il distingue les objectifs intrinsèques et extrinsèques à l'éducation, ces derniers étant plutôt des buts (aims) extérieurs au processus d'éducation, les premiers se qualifiant comme le processus de l'éducation en soi. Pour arriver à cette distinction, Graves base ses assertions sur le concept d'éducation tel que défini par Peters : « initiation into worthwhile activities » que nous pourrions traduire ainsi : initiation à des activités valables, pertinentes. Graves ajoute à la définition de l'éducation que la personne qui a été initiée à un nombre « d'activités valables » désire de son propre chef s'en approprier quelques unes (« is willing to continue with some of these on his own »).

---

[2] PROVINCE DE QUÉBEC, *Annuaire des collèges d'enseignement général et professionnel*, Québec.

[3] N. GRAVES, *Geography in Education*, London, Heinemann Educational Books Ltd., 1975, chapitre 5 : « Aims and Objectives in Geographical Education ».

Les objectifs extrinsèques sont des buts et par conséquent ne peuvent en tant que tels présider à l'élaboration d'«activités valables». Ils sont plutôt des orientations pour le professeur dans l'élaboration d'objectifs plus précis, d'activités d'apprentissage. En d'autres termes, on ne peut former un bon citoyen, mais on peut lui faire acquérir un savoir, des habilités intellectuelles, des habitudes de travail, le sens de certaines valeurs qui feront de lui un bon citoyen capable de prendre des décisions éclairées en ce qui le concerne personnellement ou encore en ce qui concerne son milieu à différentes échelles.

Appliquées à la géographie, ces « activités valables » peuvent se résumer à l'assertion suivante : « apprendre à l'élève à penser en géographe, c'est-à-dire lui apprendre la méthode géographique, les idées fondamentales de cette discipline (observation, localisation, répartition, tous genres de relations spatiales, etc.), bref des connaissances, des habiletés, des « adresses » (Bloom et Helburn).

> Bruner believes, quite rightly I think, that students should be introduced to disciplines rather than subject matter as such. It is more important that students learn to think like a geographer than it is for him to know a lot « about » the earth. Learning to think like a geographer means many things, but above all it means absorbing the conceptual structure of the discipline[4].

Au lieu de s'attarder aux objectifs de l'enseignement de la géographie urbaine au secondaire, examinons certains avantages qu'il y aurait à enseigner cette géograhie à partir des connaissances de l'élève. Un vieux principe pédagogique nous dit qu'il faut procéder du connu à l'inconnu, du concret à l'abstrait, du descriptif à l'explication[5] et nous pourrions ajouter de l'empirique au rationnel (à la classification). C'est surtout cette dernière assertion que nous voulons souligner en parlant d'abord de concept ensuite de méthode inductive.

Dire que l'élève du secondaire possède une connaissance empirique de la ville, c'est également dire qu'il possède une grande quantité de faits urbains, mais que ces faits sont confus dans son esprit. Il faut mettre de l'ordre dans ce fouillis et c'est par la « conceptualisation » qui est un processus de « catégorisation » qu'on y arrivera.

> This process benefits us in three ways. First, it reduces the complexity of the environment. Second, if gives us the means by which we identify objects in the world. Third, it reduces the necessity of constant learning[6].

Les élèves ont bien entamé un processus de « catégorisation » de leurs connaissances empiriques. Mais, ça n'a rien de systématique. C'est avec l'aide du professeur qu'ils y parviendront. Si on souhaite

---

    [4]   R. B. McNee, « Toward Stressing Structure in Geographic Instruction », in *The Social Science and Geographic Education*, sans la direction de J. M. Ball J. E. Steinbrink, J. P. Stoltman, Toronto, J. Wiley, 1971, p. 150.

    [5]   P. Boden, *Developments in Geography Teaching*, London, Open Books, 1976, p. 46.

    [6]   B. Joyce and M. Weil, *Models of Teaching*, Englewoods Cliffs, Prentice-Hall, 1972, p. 110.

tirer le maximum de cet exercice, il faut laisser les étudiants travailler par eux-mêmes.

> Expository teaching, whether oral or written, is often criticized because it masks from students the nature (attributes) of the concepts which are being taught[7].

C'est à l'étudiant à ce stade-ci du cours, de découvrir les différentes facettes d'un concept. Par exemple, qu'est-ce que le thème «le changement» implique dans la ville? Au début, l'étudiant aura des images concrètes et un petit nombre du changement. Mais peu à peu, grâce à son travail, il agrandira le champ du changement pour en arriver à catégoriser et à pouvoir établir une certaine synthèse du changement. Le changement lui apparaîtra alors sous beaucoup de facettes et de plus il se rendra compte qu'il est une caractéristique de la ville moderne. Pour cela, il faut prendre le temps nécessaire. Nous pourrions encore citer l'exemple du thème «le transport». Nous arriverions aux mêmes conclusions. Ce qui importe dans tout ce travail, ce n'est pas tellement le résultat, mais les habilités qui conduisent au résultat; à notre avis, elles comptent parmi les «activités valables» de Peters.

La méthode inductive (et ses nombreuses formes) nous semble tout indiqué au secondaire lorsque l'épistémologie des sciences enseignées le permet. Neville Scarfe, parlant de géographie, disait à peu près ceci lors d'une causerie à Toronto en 1975: «La méthode inductive, c'est pour le secondaire tandis que la méthode déductive c'est pour l'université.» De plus, McNee, toujours au sujet de la géographie, apporte la précision suivante: «Bruner believes that the inductive approach is the most effective method of developping this conceptual structure in the mind of the student[8].» Nous avons toujours été convaincu que la méthode déductive vient en deuxième lieu au secondaire et particulièrement en préparation à l'université. Pourquoi? La méthode déductive partira d'une loi, d'une théorie, d'une généralisation et.c, et en prouvera la véracité en l'appliquant à des exemples choisis. Or, il faut un «background» géographique pour bien suivre le raisonnement déductif. Est-ce que l'élève du secondaire possède ce «background» pour qu'on puisse utiliser abondamment cette méthode? Nous ne le croyons pas. Il faut d'abord lui permettre de constituer cette somme de connaissances, ce «background». La méthode inductive s'y prêtera mieux: observation (cueillette de données), classification, élaboration d'hypothèses, vérification des hypothèses, etc. De plus, c'est la méthode qui permettra d'utiliser au mieux les connaissances des élèves, de raffiner, de préciser leurs concepts. Plusieurs techniques d'apprentissage se prêtent à cette fin. Qu'il nous suffise d'en énumérer quelques unes pour illustrer diverses

---

[7] *Idem*, p. 117.

[8] R. B. McNee, «Toward Stressing Structure in Geographic Instruction», in *The Social Science and Geographic Education*, sans la direction de J. M. Ball, J. E. Steinbrink, J. P. Soltman, Toronto, J. Wiley, 1971, p. 150.

façons d'amener les élèves à exprimer leurs connaissances de la ville : une rédaction sur sa ville, un questionnaire à remplir, l'expression orale ou écrite de leurs intérêts, la cartographie de l'utilisation du sol d'un quartier de la ville, des rapports d'excursion, des relevés par des techniques d'enquête : questionnaires, interviews, l'étude d'un thème particulier, individuellement ou en groupe, par simulation, par des recherches personnelles, par l'analyse de photos, etc. C'est ainsi que pourrait débuter le cours.

Nous terminerons en décrivant brièvement le programme-cadre « Urban Studies » du ministère de l'Éducation de l'Ontario. Plusieurs idées exprimées dans le présent article proviennent de ce programme-cadre. Il est très bien fait : les objectifs sont bien pensés, le contenu est bien adapté à des élèves de 12 ans de scolarité, les méthodes suggérées sont de nature à aider l'élève dans son développement intellectuel. En somme, et son titre l'indique, il donne une optique qui en plus de permettre un enseignement géographique, pourra engager l'interdisciplinarité et favoriser le développement d'une culture urbaine.

Trois grandes parties, subdivisées en treize thèmes, structurent le contenu (traduction de l'auteur) :

1 — la ville moderne :
   a) le changement,
   b) la lutte pour l'espace,
   c) le transport,
   d) les groupes humains,
   e) le coût de la croissance;
2 — la croissance et la raison d'être des villes :
   a) la raison d'être des villes,
   b) les fonctions urbaines,
   c) la ville et la région,
   d) la hiérarchie urbaine,
   e) le changement dans le réseau urbain;
3 — l'urbanisation et la société :
   a) l'urbanisation,
   b) les villes primatiales,
   c) la ville de l'avenir.

Mentionnons que chaque partie, après une brève description, est accompagnée d'une liste de sujets d'étude dont plusieurs peuvent être convertis en travaux pratiques.

Dans le contenu que nous venons d'énumérer, nous distinguons trois niveaux qui correspondent aux trois parties. D'abord, un niveau concret se référant au factuel : la ville moderne. C'est évidemment à ce niveau que viendrait se situer les premiers travaux du cours dont il a été question plus haut, travaux qui partent des connaissances des élèves. Ils pourraient aboutir à la description et à l'explication d'un des cinq thèmes ou encore à d'autres. Le deuxième niveau se situe à un degré d'abstraction plus élevé ; il est la continuation du premier.

Le cours, ici, utilise encore la méthode inductive mais avec la différence qu'il est dirigé vers la compréhension de concepts précis: les données sont fournies à l'élève qui découvre un «modèle», une généralisation, une théorie. Ainsi, par exemple, pour comprendre la théorie de Christaller, les théories de la croissance urbaine ou encore les fonctions urbaines, le professeur munira ses élèves de données de base et orientera les travaux. Le troisième niveau coiffe et intègre les deux premiers tout en élargissant le cadre des études au monde. L'enseignement serait encore plus dirigé et pourrait même comprendre des cours magistraux. Cependant, l'étude du dernier thème, «la ville de l'avenir», pourrait être la responsabilité des élèves. Ainsi, le cours aurait commencé par eux et se terminerait par eux.

L'ordre dans lequel cet article suggère de couvrir les thèmes insiste sur l'emploi des connaissances empiriques des élèves, l'emploi de la méthode inductive. Cependant, plusieurs raisons peuvent motiver un ordre différent : le style d'enseignement du professeur, ses qualifications, la situation de l'école, le temps alloué, etc. Toutefois, il nous semble que la structure du contenu met l'accent sur la méthode inductive surtout qu'on peut greffer à celle-ci, au point de départ, les connaissances de l'élève.

Bref, cet article a voulu souligner les avantages qu'il y a de partir des connaissances des élèves; n'oublions pas que ce sont des élèves du secondaire, cycle sénior. Il est évident que ce procédé n'est pas facile, qu'il demande un professeur expérimenté. Mais, ce faisant l'élève n'est pas considéré comme une «cruche à remplir», ses connaissances deviennent un actif, l'intensité lumineuse de certains buts augmente, certaines méthodes d'enseignement s'imposent comme mieux adaptées à des élèves du secondaire, un contenu approprié se profile. Il nous semble que le programme-cadre «Urban Studies» est de nature à alimenter les réflexions en ce sens.

HIÉRARCHIE D'APPRENTISSAGE ET STRUCTURATION D'UN CONTENU À ENSEIGNER EN GÉOGRAPHIE

Monique Lapointe-Aubin, Ph.D.

Ministère de l'Éducation
Province de Québec

INTRODUCTION

La carte est un mode d'expression et de communication indispensable à l'enseignement de la géographie, et parmi les diverses cartes, la carte topographique, particulièrement utile à l'étudiant, offre de nombreuses possibilités pédagogiques. Néanmoins, parmi les notions fondamentales nécessaires à son utilisation, il semble que la notion de représentation du relief par des courbes de niveau présente encore, de nos jours, quelques difficultés didactiques mal identifiées.

C'est dans le but notamment de répondre aux problèmes rencontrés dans l'enseignement et l'apprentissage de cette notion importante que nous avons élaboré une thèse de doctorat intitulée « Construction et évaluation d'un cours programmé sur la représentation cartographique du relief en secondaire I » (Lapointe-Aubin, 1975).

Différentes étapes, toutes aussi fondamentales les unes que les autres, caractérisent notre recherche et l'objet de cet exposé est de vous décrire l'une de ces étapes importantes, soit la structuration du contenu à enseigner au moyen d'une hiérarchie d'apprentissage. Cependant, pour une meilleure compréhension du sujet traité, qu'il me soit permis de vous présenter, en premier lieu, un bref résumé de l'ensemble de la recherche.

I.—RÉSUMÉ DE LA RECHERCHE

Une expérience de plusieurs années dans l'enseignement de la géographie nous a fait constater, à l'instar de quelques autres didacticiens de différents pays, que la notion de représentation du relief par des courbes de niveau semble mal assimilée par les étudiants et difficile à enseigner par le professeur.

Ce double problème d'apprentissage et d'enseignement repose, semble t il sur la complexité des opérations mentales mises en cause, concepts et règles notamment; il provient aussi, entre autres, du nombre élevé d'étudiants dans les classes et des techniques d'enseignement souvent inadaptées aux besoins.

Le but de notre recherche a donc été de construire six unités d'enseignement individualisé programmé, de les expérimenter et de les évaluer en fonction d'un autre type d'enseignement couramment utilisé, le cours traditionnel. À notre avis, pour maîtriser les concepts et les habiletés complexes nécessaires à l'étude de la courbe de niveau, le cours programmé est plus efficace que le cours traditionnel parce qu'il se fonde sur le respect du rythme individuel, sur un emploi systématique du renforcement, sur la participation de l'étudiant, sur une structuration rigoureusement hiérarchisée, sur une micrograduation du contenu, sur l'énoncé et l'évaluation des objectifs de comportement, sur l'utilisation d'un matériel pédagogique scientifiquement expérimenté et évaluée, etc.

Construites d'après les principes précités, les unités d'enseignement et d'apprentissage individualisés ont été ensuite expérimentées et corrigées à plusieurs reprises. L'instrument de mesure validé auprès d'étudiants et de professeurs a servi à évaluer l'atteinte des objectifs du programme, situés principalement au niveau de l'apprentissage de concepts et de règles.

Dans le but d'évaluer ce matériel pédagogique, une expérimentation, menée en milieu scolaire, a vérifié quatre hypothèses formulées relativement à l'apprentissage obtenu au postest, à la rétention des notions acquises, au Q.I. et au sexe des étudiants. L'expérimentation, exigeant 12 périodes d'enseignement réparties sur trois semaines, a été menée dans vingt classes de secondaire I, auprès de 523 étudiants. Partagés en trois groupes, chacun a été soumis au hasard aux traitements suivants : traitement T_2, prétest, enseignement programmé, postest et test de rétention; traitement T_2, prétest, enseignement traditionnel, postest et test de rétention; traitement T_3, prétest et postest seulement.

Pour vérifier les hypothèses formulées, on a appliqué une analyse de covariance. L'analyse des résultats a permis de constater une différence significative entre les résultats d'apprentissage au postest en faveur des étudiants ayant utilisé le programme. Il en a été de même au test de rétention. De plus, il y a eu une interaction entre le Q.I. ainsi que le sexe des étudiants et les méthodes d'enseignement utilisées.

Cette évaluation manifeste donc l'efficacité relative des unités d'enseignement et d'apprentissage individualisés que nous avons produites. Ce matériel didactique[1] permettra, nous l'espérons, de mettre à la disposition des étudiants et des professeurs du secondaire un instrument de travail susceptible d'assurer l'auto-apprentissage de notions importantes de la géographie.

---

[1]   Actuellement sous presse, Québec, Éditions françaises.

II. — TECHNIQUE DE STRUCTURATION UTILISÉE

A. Description de la technique

Pour la structuration du contenu à enseigner, nous avons utilisé une technique québécoise, mise au point par le professeur Robert Brien de l'Université Laval (1972) et inspirée principalement de la hiérarchie d'apprentissage de Gagné (1965) et de l'algorithme d'enseignement de Landa (1962), 1974).

Pour Gagné, l'analyse de tâche en vue d'un apprentissage est une activité de planification très importante. Ce dernier désigne, *par hiérarchie*, un ensemble d'habiletés ayant une relation entre elles selon un ordre de subordination et qui sont considérées comme des préalables à l'apprentissage d'une tâche finale. Ces habiletés sont disposées hiérarchiquement selon les différents types d'apprentissage établis par l'auteur. De la subordination des habiletés acquises, il doit résulter un transfert positif vertical d'un apprentissage subordonné à un apprentissage supérieur.

Pour le professeur Landa, cette activité de planification par l'analyse du contenu joue également un rôle important dans le processus d'enseignement et d'apprentissage. Il définit l'algorithme comme une procédure finie, un ensemble de règles, qui permet de résoudre une classe donnée de problèmes. Son principal souci est d'arriver à découvrir et à développer chez l'élève des mécanismes psychologiques internes exacts, suffisamment généralisés et efficaces dans le but de produire et d'assurer un comportement donné.

Ainsi, pour Landa, l'algorithme d'enseignement est un *modèle* qui favorise une démarche de généralisation, empruntant ainsi la logique de l'algorithme mathématique.

D'après Landa, si l'on parvient à découvrir ces structures internes des mécanismes de la pensée, leur représentation au moyen d'algorithmes constituera des modèles indispensables à l'élaboration de tout programme d'enseignement.

Ainsi, à la lumière de ces données, la technique québécoise que nous avons utilisée s'inspire à la fois de la hiérarchie d'apprentissage et de l'algorithme d'enseignement. La technique consiste, en premier lieu, à écrire le diagramme logique du cheminement de celui qui maîtrise un algorithme. À partir de ce diagramme, il s'agit ensuite de faire un relevé des règles, des concepts et des sous-concepts nécessaires à ce cheminement. Ces différents types d'information prennent le nom de schèmes qui sont de deux sortes : les schèmes-représentations (concept, règle, image) et les schèmes-opérations (règle et algorithme). Ce sont ces différents schèmes qui, interreliés et hiérarchisés en règles et en concepts, permettent d'élaborer l'arborescence des schèmes requis pour maîtriser un algorithme d'enseignement. Pour le professeur Brien : « Structurer un cours, c'est construire l'arborescence des schèmes que l'étudiant devrait avoir acquis à la fin du cours » (1972, page 19). Ainsi, l'arborescence des schèmes, une fois construite, indique clairement au professeur les schèmes qu'il doit enseigner et dans quel ordre il peut le faire.

Dans le but de faire acquérir à l'étudiant les différents schèmes, il faut lui fournir une information extérieure, c'est-à-dire un contenu informatif idéal (c.i.i.). Si l'étudiant acquiert un schème quelconque, il sera par la suite en mesure de le démontrer dans un comportement adéquat; par exemple, s'il a acquis une règle, il sera capable de l'appliquer. Ainsi, le ou les objectifs de comportement, relatifs à chaque schème de l'arborescence, peuvent être énoncés et peuvent servir à vérifier si les schèmes enseignés ont été assimilés.

B. Construction de l'arborescence des schèmes du programme

Nous décrirons maintenant la démarche de structuration que nous avons suivie pour notre propre programme. Nous avons d'abord déterminé les schèmes requis par le cours programmé; nous avons apporté, avec l'assentiment de l'auteur, quelques modifications, comme le démontre le tableau suivant.

Tableau 1

Schèmes utilisés par le programme
sur la représentation cartographique de relief

Schèmes	schèmes-représentations	concept concret (c) concept défini (c)
	schèmes-opérations	règle (ro) algorithme (A)

Nous avons ensuite construit l'arborescence des schèmes requis par notre programme sur la courbe de niveau, en suivant la démarche décrite dans le diagramme logique du tableau 2.

À partir du diagramme logique du tableau 2, voici la description des étapes que nous avons franchies pour élaborer l'arborescence des schèmes requis à la maîtrise de l'algorithme du programme.

(1) Détermination de l'objectif de comportement terminal
La première démarche de structuration a consisté à déterminer l'objectif de comportement terminal du programme. Cet objectif contient les deux éléments complémentaires suivants:

a) La connaissance, la compréhension et l'application des notions de base sur la représentation cartographique du relief, qui doivent être ancrées dans la structure cognitive de l'étudiant. Cette phase comprend principalement des exercices de mémorisation, de compréhension et d'application concernant la lecture du relief par la courbe de niveau.

b) L'initiation au commentaire du relief dans le but de faire saisir à l'étudiant certaines relations qui existent entre les activités de l'homme et le relief terrestre, représentés sur une carte topographique à grande échelle. Cette phase qui en est une de révision et de synthèse, permet l'utilisation des connaissances et des habiletés acquises.

L'objectif de comportement terminal du programme s'énonce donc ainsi :

Étant donné une carte topographique canadienne à grande échelle, l'étudiant de Secondaire I sera capable de lire et de commenter de façon élémentaire, le relief représenté au moyen de la courbe de niveau.

②et③ Le schème qui correspond à l'objectif de comportement terminal que nous avons formulé est un algorithme, c'est-à-dire qu'il est constitué d'un ensemble de règles-opérations, favorisant une démarche de généralisation.

④ Nous avons alors construit le diagramme logique de l'algorithme de la représentation cartographique du relief. Le tableau 3 suivant contient ce diagramme.

⑤⑥⑦⑧Le contenu informatif idéal (c.i.i.) des règles et des concepts de l'algorithme a été ensuite écrit et un symbole (concept (c), règle (ro), algorithme (A)) a été attribué à chaque schème, tels qu'ils sont définis dans les feuillets d'analyse suivantes :

Feuille d'analyse

Énoncés et défininitions (c.i.i.)

Symboles

A_1*   (Algorithme composé de ro1, ro2, ro3, ro4, ro5).

ro1   Dans la représentation du relief d'une carte topographique, si l'on désire connaître l'altitude d'un endroit précis de la carte, on trouve l'altitude à partir d'une courbe de niveau cotée.

ro2   Dans la représentation du relief d'une carte topographique, si l'on désire une coupe de terrain d'un endroit précis de la carte, on exécute le profil topographique à partir des courbes de niveau représentant cet endroit.

ro3   Dans la représentation du relief d'une carte topographique, si l'on désire connaître quelle pente représentent certaines courbes de niveau, on trouve si ces courbes représentent une pente faible, forte, régulière, concave ou convexe.

ro4   Dans la représentation du relief d'une carte topographique, si l'on désire connaître quelle forme de terrain représentent certaines courbes de niveau, on trouve si ces courbes représentent une colline, une vallée, un col, une plaine, un plateau ou une montagne.

ro5   Dans la représentation du relief d'une carte topographique, si l'on désire analyser l'influence exercée par le relief sur un phénomène précis de la carte, on exécute le commentaire de carte relatif à ce phénomène.

ro1   c1   La courbe de niveau est une ligne qui joint tous les points situés à la même altitude au-dessus du niveau moyen des mers.

ro6   On obtient l'altitude d'une courbe de niveau cotée en trouvant sa valeur numérique d'altitude sur la courbe.

ro7   On obtient l'altitude d'une courbe de niveau non cotée, en additionnant l'équidistance à la courbe de niveau cotée, de plus basse altitude.

---

*À noter qu'il est possible de décomposer un algorithme en sous-algorithme pour en arriver aux ro (règles-opérations) qui sont, en fait, de petits algorithmes.

Tableau 2

DIAGRAMME LOGIQUE DE L'AUTEUR QUI ÉLABORE UNE ARBORESCENCE*

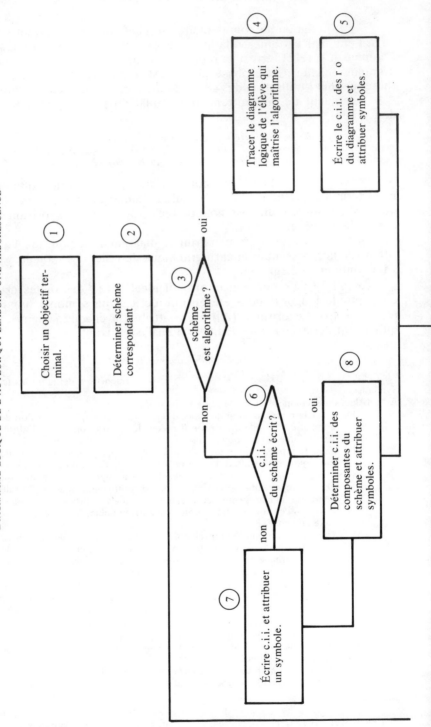

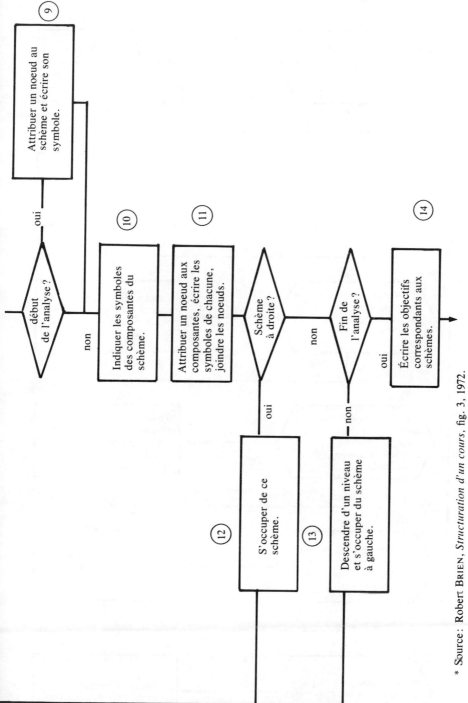

* Source : Robert BRIEN, *Structuration d'un cours*, fig. 3, 1972.

Tableau 3

DIAGRAMME LOGIQUE DE L'ALGORITHME SUR LE REPRÉSENTATION CARTOGRAPHIQUE DU RELIEF

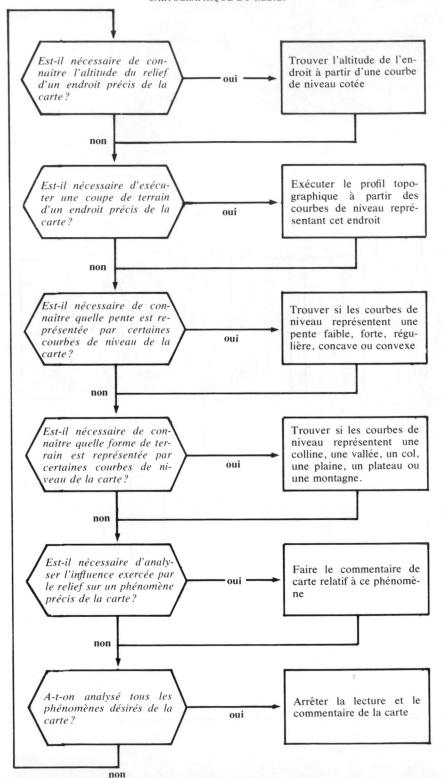

	ro8	On obtient l'altitude d'un endroit situé entre deux courbes de niveau, en calculant approximativement sa distance entre les deux courbes de niveau.
ro2	c1	Courbe de niveau : acquise.
	c12	Profil topographique : coupe du terrain.
	ro10	Éxécution du profil topographique.
ro3	c1	Courbe de niveau : acquise.
	c13	Pente : inclinaison du sol par rapport à l'horizon.
	ro11	Sur la carte topographique, analyser si la disposition des courbes de niveau représentent une pente faible, forte, régulière, concave ou convexe.
ro4	c1	Courbe de niveau : acquise.
	ro12	Sur une carte topographique, analyser si la disposition des courbes de niveau représente une colline, une vallée, un col, une plaine, un plateau ou une montagne.
ro5	c1	Courbe de niveau : acquise.
	ro11	Représentation d'une pente : acquise.
	ro12	Représentation d'une forme de terrain : acquise.
	ro13	Établir la relation entre le relief terrestre et des cours d'eau représentés sur la carte.
	ro14	Établir la relation entre le relief et certains phénomènes urbains représentés sur la carte.
	ro15	Établir la relation entre le relief et quelques phénomènes de communication terrestre.
	ro16	Établir la relation entre le relief et le développement des zones agricoles.
	ro17	Établir la relation entre le relief et la pratique de divers sports.
c1	c2	Carte topographique : pré-requis.
	c3	Relief terrestre : pré-requis
	c4	Niveau moyen des mers : niveau de référence où aboutissent les cours d'eau.
	c5	Altitude : élévation verticale d'un point au-dessus du N.M.M.
ro6	c5	Altitude : acquise.
	c6	Courbe de niveau cotée : courbe maîtresse qui porte une valeur numérique d'élévation.
ro7	c5	Altitude : acquise.
	c7	Courbe de niveau non cotée : courbe intermédiaire qui ne contient généralement, aucune valeur numérique d'élévation.
	c8	Équidistance : différence d'altitude constante entre deux courbes de niveau qui se suivent.
	ro9	On obtient l'équidistance des courbes de niveau en la lisant au bas de la carte ou en soustrayant deux courbes de niveau cotées l'une par rapport à l'autre et en divisant cette différence par le nombre de tranches qui s'y trouvent.
ro8	c5	Altitude : acquise.
	c8	Équidistance : acquise.
ro11	c14	Pente faible : pente dont les courbes sont espacées les unes des autres.
	c15	Pente forte : pente dont les courbes sont rapprochées les unes des autres.
	c16	Pente régulière : pente dont les courbes sont également espacées les unes des autres.
	c17	Pente concave : pente dont les courbes sont rapprochées au haut de la pente et sont espacées au bas de la pente.
	c18	Pente convexe : pente dont les courbes sont espacées au haut de la pente et sont rapprochées au bas de la pente.
ro12	c19	Colline : relief d'altitude croissante, dont les courbes sont généralement disposées en cercle.
	c20	Vallée : relief dont les courbes disposées parallèlement ou en V, décroissent en altitude.
	c21	Col : relief dont les courbes représentent une dépression entre deux sommets ou de montagnes.
	c22	Plaine : relief dont les courbes sont espacées les unes des autres.

	c23	Plateau : relief dont les courbes de niveau représentent une surface plus ou moins ondulée et un rebord généralement disséqué.
	c24	Montagne : relief de haute altitude dont les courbes sont nombreuses et rapprochées.
c2	c9	Signes conventionnels : pré-requis.
	c10	Échelle de la carte : pré-requis.
	c11	Coordonnées de la carte : pré-requis.

⑨ Nous avons ensuite disposé les schèmes ainsi formulés, en tableau (page suivante). Comme il s'agit du début de l'analyse, nous avons assigné un noeud au schème de l'objectif de comportement terminal et nous lui avons attribué le symbole A, pour algorithme, tel que l'indique la première ligne de l'arborescence du tableau 4 suivant.

⑩ Les symboles des composantes du schème A ont été indiqués dans une brochette de petits carrés, comme l'indique la première ligne du tableau 4.

⑪ Un noeud a été attribué à chacune de ces composantes qui apparaissent en deuxième ligne du tableau 4. Le symbole de chacune a été écrit et les nœuds ont été reliés les uns aux autres par des lignes droites.

⑫ Nous avons fait une analyse de même genre pour chaque schème situé sur la deuxième ligne, en allant vers la droite (voir tableau 4).

⑬ Une analyse semblable a été faite pour chacun des schèmes de la troisième ligne, puis de la quatrième ligne, à partir de la gauche (voir tableau 4).

⑭ Puis les objectifs de comportement correspondant à chaque schème de l'arborescence ont été formulés.

L'arborescence des schèmes du tableau 4, a permis ensuite de diviser le contenu à programmer en six leçons hiérarchisées, tel que présenté dans le tableau 5 de la page suivante. Toutes les leçons du programme se trouvent hiérarchisées. Chaque leçon contient également une hiérarchie de sous-notions qu'il s'agissait de rédiger méthodiquement, en suivant l'ordre dans lequel ces schèmes doivent être enseignés et acquis, c'est-à-dire, de bas en haut, et de gauche à droite de l'arborescence. Par exemple, la notion de carte topographique (c2) est un préalable, l'enseignement débute avec les notions de relief terrestre (c3) et de niveau moyen des mers (c4), suivies de celle de l'altitude (c5) qui forment les composantes du concept de courbe de niveau (c1), etc.; ce dernier, à son tour, sert à l'acquisition des cinq règles majeures du programme, soit : ro1, ro2, ro3, ro4 et ro5, et ainsi de suite (voir tableau 4).

Les deux premières leçons servent de préalables essentiels aux quatre autres leçons du programme. Pour sa part, la sixième leçon sert à réviser et à appliquer toutes les notions importantes du programme au moyen d'une carte topographique à grande échelle : en outre, elle établit certaines relations qui existent entre les réalisations humaines et le relief terrestre représenté sur cette carte. Le tableau 5 décrit le contenu de six leçons du programme.

Tableau 4

ARBORESCENCE DES SCHÈMES REQUIS À LA MAÎTRISE DE L'ALGORITHME
SUR LA REPRÉSENTATION CARTOGRAPHIQUE DU RELIEF

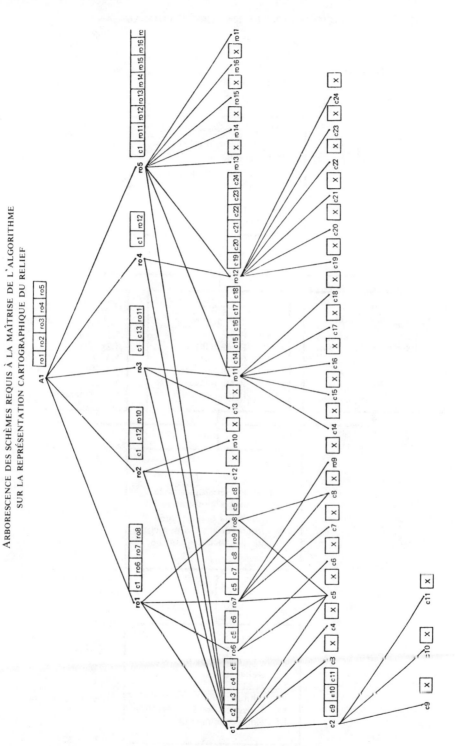

Tableau 5

HIÉRARCHIE DU CONTENU DU PROGRAMME SUR LA REPRÉSENTATION
CARTOGRAPHIQUE DU RELIEF

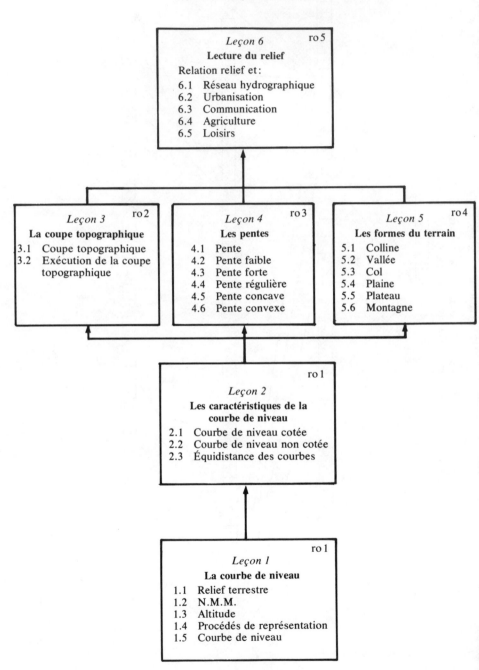

C. Planification du processus d'enseignement

L'arborescence des schèmes requis pour la maîtrise de l'algorithme sur la représentation du relief nous a donc permis de connaître et de planifier les étapes suivantes, avant le début de notre enseignement :

1. L'ensemble des schèmes (règles et concepts) qu'un étudiant devra avoir acquis à la fin du programme et l'ordre dans lequel il les assimilera.
2. L'objectif relatif à chaque schème, énonçant le comportement qui est attendu de l'étudiant après la session d'enseignement.
2. Le type d'apprentissage auquel renvoie chaque schème du programme.
4. Les conditions internes et externes d'apprentissage inhérentes à chaque type d'apprentissage (selon Gagné).
5. Les événements d'enseignement relatifs à chaque schème; dans notre programme, ils sont nombreux et variés. Mentionnons, entre autres, la communication à l'étudiant des objectifs avant chaque leçon; la conception de cinquante-six illustrations cartographiques dans le but de favoriser l'attention, la découverte et la compréhension des notions enseignées; deux bandes illustrées sur des notions de base; une carte topographique permettant l'exécution de travaux pratiques; etc.
6. Les préalables nécessaires à l'acquisition et au transfert de chaque schème requis pour la tâche finale.
7. L'évaluation de la maîtrise de chaque schème par l'étudiant, au moyen d'un test d'évaluation dont au moins une question porte sur chacun des objectifs, en fonction de son type d'apprentissage. Ce test totalise 40 questions objectives et 2 questions traditionnelles d'application.
8. Après l'enseignement, en cas d'échec, l'identification du (ou des) schème(s) que l'étudiant ne maîtrise pas.

CONCLUSION

Par le choix de ce modèle de structuration du contenu à enseigner, nous avons voulu optimaliser un processus d'apprentissage qui vise principalement l'acquisition des habiletés intellectuelles sous-jacentes à la notion de représentation du relief par des courbes de niveau. Ce modèle de hiérarchisation du contenu nous permet de constater la complexité des opérations mentales requises à l'apprentissage de cette notion importante de la carte topographique. À notre avis, en géographie et indépendamment de la discipline, nombre d'autres notions présentent aussi des problèmes d'enseignement et d'apprentissage et auraient grand avantage à recevoir ainsi une attention très particulière.

BIBLIOGRAPHIE

BRIEN, R., *Structuration d'un cours (rapport technique)*. Québec, Université Laval, Département de la technologie de l'enseignement, 1972.

GAGNÉ, R., *The Conditions of Learning*, New York, Holt, Rinehart & Winston, 1965.

GAGNÉ, R., *Essentials of Learning for Instruction*. Hinsdale, Illinois, The Dryden Press, 1974.

LANDA, L. N., *Recherche sur l'application de la logique mathématique et de la théorie de l'information à quelques problèmes d'enseignement. Enseignement programmé*, Paris, 1962, pp. 61-65.

LANDA, L. N., *Algorithmization in Learning and Instruction*, Educational Technologie Publication, 1974. Englewood Cliffs, New Jersey.

LAPOINTE-AUBIN, M., *Construction et évaluation d'un cours programmé sur la représentation cartographique du relief en secondaire I*, Thèse de PH.D., Université de Montréal, Faculté des Sciences de l'Éducation, 1975.

RESEARCH IN GEOGRAPHICAL EDUCATION

JOHN WOLFORTH
McGill University

Among the various branches of geography, geographical education has the most weakly defined research dimension. Other branches, of both physical and human geography, rely on research for their continued growth, and few would be taught today at university level in ways that are not radically different from those in which they were taught a generation ago.[1] Most have changed almost beyond recognition. This is not so of courses in geographical education, the 'methods' courses of university Faculties of Education, where much of the content concerning pedagogical skills specific to geography, such as the interpretation of topographical maps, aerial photographs, diagrams and graphs, is still more or less the standard fare of geographical educators of a previous generation. Some new skills have been added to the geography teacher's bag of tricks, including games and simulations or the interpretation of Landsat imagery, but geographical education has not yet been transformed by research and epistemological debate in the same way as has, say, urban geography.

It is symptomatic, perhaps, that there is no distinctive way to describe those who are specialists in the transmission of geographical knowledge and whose research is focussed on this area. "Teacher trainers" is too crude and circumscribed a description of their role, whilst the more usual "geographical educators" is too comprehensive. Arc not all, indeed, "geographical educators", from the primary school teacher exploring with his class the local community to the specialist in periglacial processes leading her graduate seminar? For the sake of greater precision, the French practice of using the term "geographical didactics" might, although cumbersome in translation, provide a more distinctive way of describing what such people see as their field of interest. However, let it not be supposed that the use of a distinctive label would of itself ensure the development of a distinctive and respectable research dimension.

The reason for the poor development of research in geographical didactics are numerous. First, those who practice this branch of geography in the universities often do not perceive themselves as being quite the same as their colleagues in other branches. To state the po

---

[1] J. L. ROBINSON, "Geography in Canada 25 years ago", in L. E. HAMELIN and L. BEAUREGARD, *Retrospective 1951-1976* (Montreal: CAG, 1979).

sition brutally, geographical education is not seen as being very important in the hierarchy of the discipline. A recent survey, admittedly of a small and not very systematically selected cross-section of members of the Canadian Association of Geographers revealed that, while:

> to encourage the advance of geographical studies and research in Canada,

and

> To facilitate the exchange of ideas among geographers in Canada,

were seen as appropriate tasks for the Association by a large percentage of respondents, only a handful thought it was the Association's job to,

> improve the teaching of the geography of Canada. [2]

This is not to imply that many individual geographers have not made a distinguished contribution to the development of geography teaching or indeed that the Association itself, through its Education Committee, of which this present volume is just one of many contributions, has not done so. It is rather to suggest that, for many academic geographers, geographical education, or more precisely the teaching of geography in schools, is seen as something apart and to which a scientific community, committed to a common method of enquiry and reporting could make no conceivable contribution.

To some extent, there is justification for the low status of geographical education. Whilst the science of geography has experienced, with other disciplines, an almost embarrassing growth of periodical literature, it is remarkable that in neither English nor French are there journals devoted exclusively to reporting research in geographical didactics, the one possible exception being *Geographical Education*, published annually by the Australian Geography Teachers' Association. There are, of course, many journals devoted to transmitting teaching ideas to teachers, such as, to take Canadian examples, Ontario's *Monograph* or Quebec's *Géographie didactique* and *Geoscope*. But the ideas presented in such journals are rarely if ever, informed by research. They are merely good "recipes" which innovative practitioners have found to work in their own classrooms.

Part of the problem undoubtedly arises from a practical consideration concerning the ambivalent role of geographical educators in Canadian Universities. The sixties was a decade of unparalleled quantitative growth in Canadian education, of frantic school-building programs to accommodate the children of the post-war baby boom, and of accelerated demand for new teachers. Many new appointments were made to the geography departments of University Faculties of

---

[2]   H. A. WHITNEY and L. BUREAU, "The CAG as seen by its members", in L. E. HAMELIN AND L. BEAUREGARD, *op. cit.*

Education at the time and those who came did so either with research experience and academic qualifications in other areas (such as curriculum theory or a geographical specialism other than didactics) or with no research experience at all. Many of those who were appointed at this time had demonstrated their competence as superior classroom teachers rather than as researchers. Moreover, in the early years of such appointments it was often difficult to redress the imbalance between practice and research: time and energy was simply too absorbed in turning out yet more and more teachers with the basic survival kit of classroom skills to engage in introspection. The skills that were transmitted were consequently the tried and true, the conventional wisdom of geographical education's own particular folk tradition.

However, all this has shown signs of changing. The present volume shows some evidence of the variety of research activities being engaged in by Canadian professional geographical educators, and while no Canadian university yet offers a formal doctoral program in geographical education *per se*, a growing number of theses, dissertations, and projects attest to the burgeoning research activity in Canada at the level of the Master's degree.[3]

The purpose of this essay then is to try to draw together some loose threads, to attempt to clarify what is meant by research in the didactics of geography and how it may be different from research in geography itself. And to suggest possible avenues for such research, some of which are being actively followed.

I—GEOGRAPHY AS SCIENCE AND AS DIDACTICS

It is first necessary to draw a distinction between the function of scientific geography, as reflected in the content of University courses and scholarly writing, and the functions of geography as a subject in the school curriculum. At one time, when regional geography reigned supreme, there was a considerable conformity between them, and school geography could rightly be seen as a watered down version of the pure spirit served up at university. Even later, at the height of the so-called quantitative revolution, the innovative approaches in school geography which motivated such British books as *Frontiers in Geographical Teaching*[4] and *New Directions in Geography*[5] bor-

[3] H. DHAND, *Research in Social Studies Education at Canadian Universities* (Saskatoon: Research Resources Centre, College of Education, University of Saskatchewan, 1979). Although now somewhat dated, M. C. NAISH, *Some Aspects of the Study and Teaching of Geography in Britain and a Review of Recent British Research* (Sheffield: Geographical Association, 1972); and R. N. SAVELAND and C. W. PANNELL, *Inventory of Recent U.S. Research in Geographic Education* (Athens, Ga.: University of Georgia, 1975), both provide useful comparisons for the U.K. and the U.S.A. respectively.

[4] R. J. CHORLEY and P. HAGGETT (eds.)., *Frontier in Geographical Teaching* (London; Methuen, 1965).

[5] R. WALFORD (ed.), *New Directions in Geography Teaching* (London: Longmans, 1973).

rowed from a methodology which had galvanized geographical research. Today it is much harder to detect points of similarity, and the gap between geography at school and university does indeed appear to be growing.[6] This is especially evident in Canada where a survey of provincial curricula like that carried out by Jones in this volume and elsewhere[7] reveals that geography courses are founded either upon a regional base, or upon one which draws from an interdisciplinary, problem-centred approach. In contrast, university courses are more obviously rooted in one or other systematic branch of the discipline.

Consequently, in Canada as elsewhere, geographical education cannot be seen as simply the process of transmitting at the level of the school child a distillation of the body of knowledge which goes under the name of geography at the University. That this can still be an important component of geographical education is shown by the useful work carried out at the Information and Documentation Centre for the Geography of the Netherlands in Utrecht, where a model has been developed showing how information generated by the *science* of geography may be translated into materials and related activities suitable for the *didactics* for geography.[8] This kind of work, drawing its inspiration from Bruner's dictum that it is possible to teach anything in some intellectually satisfying way to a child at any level, has undoubted usefulness for many kinds of geographical output, particularly that of a substantive nature. Increasingly, however, much of what might be called frontier research in geography is either of doubtful relevance to the classroom, or involves analytical techniques which loose their impact if presented in an abbreviated or simplified form, a point which will be elaborated later.

In physical geography, the shift towards the study of process, often involving quantitative analysis over a long period, removed, without putting anything in its place, the solid, eminently teachable credibility of Davisian morphological models. It is only recently that process-based textbooks have appeared at the University level, let alone that of the secondary school.[9] In human geography, the situation is even cloudier, for loss of confidence in the epistemology of logical positivism has resulted in a divergence of approaches, on the one hand towards those have a stated political commitment, and on the other towards those that are based upon introspection and subjec-

---

    6 A. KIRBY and D. LAMBERT, *Geography at School and University : Is the Gap Between them Growing* ? (Reading : Department of Geography, University of Reading, 1978).
    7 G. JONES, this volume; and *Geography Teaching in Canadian Schools*, (St. John's : Memorial University of Newfoundland, 1978).
    8 H. VERDUIN-MULLER *et al*, "Conceptual model for curriculum planning in geography", *Geographical Education : Curriculum Problems in Certain European Countries with Special Reference to the 16-19 Age Groups* (London : IGU Commission on Geographical Education, 1978).
    9 K. CLAYTON, "Evolution of process based geomorphology" THES, 6.6.80.

tive appraisal[10]. This has left the 'new geography' of the seventies on somewhat of a limb.

The way out of the dilemma is to try to see geography as science and geography as didactics as falling into two different categories of activity and to recognise that although didactics may draw from science when it is appropriate to do so, this will not always be the case. The difference resides in the fact that, while geography as science is directed essentially by curiosity about places or about space, depending on which side of the methodological fence one sits, geography as didactics is directed by curiosity about the learner's relationship to place and space.

To make this distinction also points the way around a criticism suggested recently by Gregory.[11] in his thought provoking but inconclusive analysis of the development of geographical thought. The approach exemplified by such projects as the American HSGP or the British GYSL, he says, is unlikely to have profound educational effects on a wide audience,

> because... even if they succeed in substituting a different image, they are still using the same camera: they remain committed to a positivist epistemology which makes social science an activity performed *on* rather than *in* society, one which portrays society but is at the same time estranged from it.

Geography as didactics is capable, if separated from geography as science, of devising ways in which students, as representatives of society interact with the environment in ways that produce learning. The task then of *research* in geographical education can be seen in broad outline as being concerned in one way or another with enquiry about the nature of this interaction.

One further distinction must be made however, between geography as science and geography as didactics, before the form this enquiry takes is elaborated upon. This is the distinction between work that is "pure" and work that is "applied". Research in geography, like that of any other science, is of its very nature "pure" in that its objective is the construction of a body of theory. This is not to say much "pure" research in geography may not be found to have practical application, or indeed that some research may not be specifically directed by the need to find a solution to some practical problem, whether in stream hydraulics or in planning. For geography as didactics, however, applied work is pre-eminent. While in geography as science, applications flow out of pure research, in geography as didactics, pure research is *directed* by the need to find and to verify better forms of application.

---

[10]   J. WOLFORTH, "The new geography —and after?" *Geography*, 61 (1976) 143-149,

[11]   D. GREGORY, *Ideology, Science and Human Geography* (London: St. Martin, 1979).

If, as in figure 1, geography as science and as didactics are portrayed in a Venn diagram, then in geography as didactics, the largest area is occupied by application. That is to say, more thought and activity will inevitably be directed towards improving instructional practice, whether in writing textbooks, participating in curriculum projects, or simply planning imaginative lessons. Nonetheless, it is important that the area representing *research* in geographical didactics should overlap that representing application and that, as far as possible, the interaction between the instructor, the learner and the subject material should be informed and guided by the findings of research. All too often in the past has it been guided by faith alone and much work remains to be done on evaluating the effectiveness of well-tried instructional strategies.

But what of the relationship between geography as didactics and other fields? Obviously, if the coherence of the discipline is worth maintaining then there must still be borrowing, and probably extensive borrowing, from academic geography. It is important that a good portion of both the content and the methodology of school geography should be derived from the geography which is reported in the research literature. If, as is often the case, geographical educators find little in that literature which seems relevant to their needs it may because geography as a science has become too arcane. Relevance to teaching might not, after all, be a bad acid test for the output of geographical research.

Besides drawing from geography as science, geography as didactics needs to look to other fields for research direction. First, the growing body of theory on how spatial learning takes place, arising from the seminal work of Piaget and Inhelder,[12] is of particular interest, if only because within academic geography, it has stimulated research on spatial behaviour in general.[13]

Secondly, the theory of curriculum development, with its roots in philosophy psychology and sociology, provides some stimulus for research in geographical didactics. Questions concerning the place of geography in the total spectrum of knowledge are of importance, if only to make clear the role that geography can play, in combination with other components of the curriculum in the learner's intellectual and social development.

In general, then, if some kind of taxonomy of research in geographical education were to be attempted, it would focus upon these interfaces:

I.   The interface between geographical education and curriculum theory.

---

[12]   J. PIAGET and B. INHELDER, *The Child's Conception of Space* (New York: Norton, 1967); and J. PIAGET, *The Child's Conception of the World* (New York: Littlefield Adams, 1963).
[13]   G. T. MOORE and R. G. GOLLEDGE (eds.), *Environmental Knowing: Theories, Research and Methods*, (Stroudsberg, Pa.: Dowden, Hutchinson and Ross, 1976).

Figure 1.   RELATIONSHIPS BETWEEN RESEARCH IN GEOGRAPHY AND
IN GEOGRAPHICAL EDUCATION.

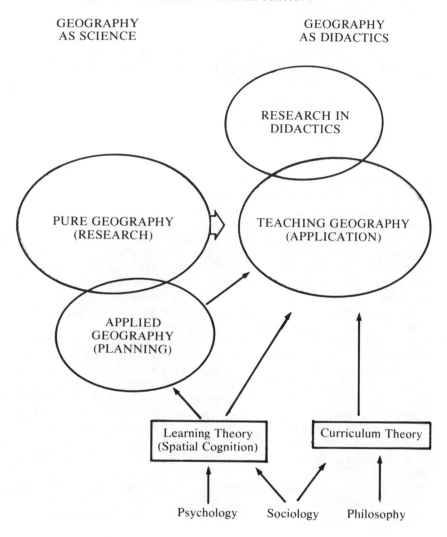

II.   The interface between geographical education and learning
theory.
III.   The interface between geography as didactics and geography as
science.

The remainder of this paper will elaborate upon the kind of research which might be undertaken in these three zones. Undoubtedly,
the catalogue will not be exhaustive but may be useful in at least
providing a map of present and future activity in the field. Since, as

has been suggested, the area of overlap between the purist's definition of research and application is a broad one, the distinction will not always be made with precision.

II—SOME DIRECTIONS FOR RESEARCH AND DEVELOPMENT IN GEOGRAPHICAL EDUCATION

A. STUDIES RELATED TO SPATIAL COGNITION

Several directions for research are apparent in the area of spatial cognition. First are questions of how children come to know space and place, and whether there are differences in spatial cognition between different groups of children (for example, between boys and girls, or between children of different cultural backgrounds). Related to these are questions of perception, which, as Dueck, points out in this volume,[14] is not the same as cognition. The child's image of the world can be considered at the microscale, where important work has been done on how children construct their own world in their local environment, worlds which may differ markedly from those of adults.[15] On the other hand, work at the macroscale has tended to focus upon children's preferred areas, in the form of so-called mental map construction.[16] For example, a recent international project of the I.G.U. has compared how children of a number of different countries rank other countries as places to live or to visit.[17] Questions which require further investigation and which arise out of work on preferential patterns, concern what children believe other places to be like, especially places they have never visited. A recent study of British childrens' images of Canada[18], although concerned more with geographical knowledge rather than perception *per se* revealed some alarming misconceptions. More cross-cultural work of this kind would be of value and would in turn give rise to other questions concerning the source of children's images of elsewhere wheter TV, travel literature, hearsay or formal teaching, and of the relative strength of these influences.

Tied in with this concern are questions of how children "make sense" of the images of place and space that are conventionally presented to them as instructional media. Milburn[19] has discussed else-

---

[14]   K. DUECK, this volume.

[15]   R. HART, *Children's Experience of Place: A Developmental Study* (New York: Halsted, 1978).

[16]   P. R. GOULD and R. WHITE, *Mental Maps*, (Harmondsworth: Penguin, 1974).

[17]   B. SPICER and F. SLATER, IGU International Perception Project, in preparation.

[18]   G. M. LEWIS, *British Students' Images of Canada*, Canada House Lecture Series No. 6 (London: Canada House, 1979).

[19]   D. MILBURN, this volume.

where in this volume how childrens' mapping abilities develop and how they can be guided, and the important work of Blaut and Stea[20] showed, in opposition to the Piagetian view of the very young child's ability to decentrate, how these abilities can be initiated by working with aerial photos and models. But what do children actually make of the small scale maps that they see in atlases and do they see the map symbolisation in the way that we, as geographically trained adults, think they see it ? One cannot but recall the oft. quoted misconception of Huckleberry Finn concerning the "colours" of the American states, a misconception shared in less extreme form by all those children who believe the green areas on the relief map indicate grasslands.

Work of this kind would provide a useful guide for application in what might be called the remedial area, since it is obviously desirable that children should have a "correct" image both of their local environment and of the wider world. At the local level, for example, Clabrough's[21] work in devising activities designed to improve the spatial abilities of so-called 'slow learners' is of interest. At the global level, if the now somewhat old-fashioned view is accepted that one at least of the tasks of geography is to teach something about other countries, then a useful starting point might be childrens' own naive preconceptions.

B.   STUDIES RELATING TO CURRICULUM THEORY

Many of the more important books which have appeared recently in the field of geographical education have been concerned with geography's role in the school curriculum.[22]

At a time when there is pressure in many places for emphasis on a "core curriculum"[23] stressing the so-called basics, geographers feel the perennial need to justify their subject's existence within the spectrum of the educational system's offerings; and this in itself has prompted some attention to curriculum theory. In addition, the influence of geography projects such as the American HSGP or the British GYSL, 14—18 and 16—19, Projects[24] has been to focus on the

---

[20]   J. M. BLAUT and D. STEA, "Studies of geographic learning", *Annals of the Association of American Geographers*, 61 (1971), 387-393.

[21]   P. CLABROUGH, *Geography and the Slow Learner*, M. Ed. monograph, McGill University, 1976.

[22]   P. BODEN, *Developments in Geography Teaching*, (London: Open Books, 1976); N. GRAVES, *Curriculum Planning in Geography* (London: Heinemann, 1979); D. HALL, *Geography and the Geography Teacher* (London: George Allen and Unwin, 1976); W. E. MARSDEN, *Evaluating the Geography Curriculum* (London: Oliver and Boyd, 1976).

[23]   See, for example, ENGLAND AND WALES, DEPT. OF EDUCATION AND SCIENCE, *A View of the Curriculum* (London: Her Majesty's Stationery Office, 1980).

[24]   The American High School Geography Project (HSGP) has recently been published in a revised edition by Macmillan, U.S.A.; The Geography for the Young School Leaver Project (GYSL) is published by Nelson; Geography 14-18 by Macmillan, U.K.; and Geography 16-19 is in the process of seeking a commercial publisher.

process of curriculum development and dissemination. Out of these two stimuli, a number of important issues have arisen.

It would certainly be beyond the scope of a short paper to enter in any substantial way into the debate on curriculum theory, except to draw attention to the implication of some of its issues to research in geographical education. Elsewhere in this volume, Jones[25] has discussed the means and model of curriculum development outlined by Tyler[26] and elaborated and operationalized by Bloom and his associates, in that bible of Canadian curriculum writers, the *Taxonomy of Educational Objectives*[27]. There is no question that this model has had strong and continuing influence on curriculum development and that it points to further research in identifying appropriate behavioural objectives for geography, as well as in developing instruments of evaluation. It is by no means a dead horse to be flogged in vain. Within geography's current post-positivistic debate concerning the discipline's role as a humanist field, or as one directed towards political action, questions concerning educational aims and objectives are very pertinent. Work could usefully be done to locate specific geographical teaching objectives along the vectors associated with aims that are related to the needs of society, those that are related to the learner's personal development and those that are determined by the structure of the disciipline itself. An analysis of existing syllabuses in these terms would be a useful guide as to which master (or combination of masters) they serve and why. Beyond this, work could also usefully be carried out on whether a relationship exists between the specific objectives of a given geography syllabus and the broader aims of the educational system to which it contributes. In a changing cultural context such as that found in developing countries, questions in this area can be especially important.[28]

But perhaps questions also need to be asked concerning the appropriateness of the means—ends model for all geographical activities. Is geography supposed to be the kind of subject Postman and Weingartner identify in their "vaccination" theory of education; namely

> a subject is something you "take" and when you have "taken" it, you have "had" it and if you have "had" it you are immune and need not take it again?[29]

[25] G. JONES, this volume.

[26] R. TYLER, *Basic Principles of Curriculum and Instruction* (Chicago : University of Chicago, 1949).

[27] B. S. BLOOM *et al* (eds.), *Taxonomy of Educational Objectives : Handbook II, The Affective Domain* (New York : Longmans Green, 1964).

[28] J. WOLFORTH and F. PHIRI, "National goals and geographical objectives", in J. S. OGURTOYIRBO *et al.* (eds.) *Resource and Development in Africa*, Vol. III (Lagos : IGU, 1978).

[29] N. POSTMAN and C. WEINGARTNER, *Teaching as a Subversive Activity* (New York : Delacarte, 1969).

Or is it predominantly a subject for which the end products are neither specific skills, nor specific knowledge, nor even specific attitudes
and values, but rather a questioning mind ? As Peters has suggested,
the key procedures, concepts and criteria of any subject are prob-
lematic, the focus of speculation rather than mastery.[30]

The handbooks for the British 14—18 Project[31] identifies three
different models of teaching style : the transmission—reception model
in which the teacher is the authoritative source of information which
is important to the pupil; the behaviour shaping model in which the
teacher is the provider of structured learning experience leading to the
achievement by the pupils of specified objectives : and the interactive
model, in which the teacher is mediator between the subject material
and the pupil, and in which teacher and pupils develop understanding
together through their mutual interaction with the subject material.
This suggests that something more like the process model of Stenhouse[32] might be an alternative yardstick to the means-ends model
against which to evaluate and develop geographical syllabuses.

In summary then, different research activities are conceivable in
the relationship between geography as didactics and curriculum
theory which, for the sake of convenience, may be grouped under the
two major models identified. These would include in a by no means
exhaustive list;

1. Means-ends model

a) The development of behavioural objectives and instruments of
   evaluation for those aspects of geographical didactics where they
   may appropriately be used (for example, map reading, interpretation) of remote sensing imagery, quantitative methods and the interpretation of geometrical models such as Horton stream
   networks or Christaller central place systems.
b) The locating of specific objectives within a map of the broader
   aims of educational systems, especially in cross-cultural comparisons.
c) The development of hierarchies of instructional activities and
   evaluative procedures related to hierarchies of objectives as
   suggested by Lapointe-Aubin in this volume.[33]

2. Process Models

a) The analysis of processes of curriculum change based either upon
   empirical historical research of the kind exemplified by Tomkins[34]

---

[30] R. S. PETERS, *Ethics and Education* (London: George Allen and Unwin,
1966).
[31] H. TOLLEY and J. B. REYNOLDS, *Geography 14-18: A Handbook for
School-Based Curriculum Development* (London: Macmillan, 1977)
[32] L. STENHOUSE, *An Introduction to Curriculum Research and Development*
(London: Heinemann, 1975).
[33] M. LAPOINTE-AUBIN, this volume.
[34] G. S. TOMKINS, this volume.

in this volume, or upon diffusion models or information systems models.

b) Studies of values and of ways of constructing curricula with the express purpose of producing attitudinal change. For example, the works of the Canada Studies Foundation had as at least an implicit aim, that pupils should more highly value things Canadian.

c) Evaluative studies investigating the procedure of existing curriculum projects and of their underlying philosophies and strategies for developments and implementation. Projects to be considered are now quite numerous and could include, besides the American HSGP, the British Schools Council's GYSL, 14-18 and 16-19 Projects mentioned above, also the Schools Council's 8-13 Social Studies Project and Environmental Studies Project, the American Earth Science Curriculum Project, the German RCFP, the Dutch Participation Project Randstadt, the Australian SGEP, and others.

Not falling easily under either of the two headings identified above are research questions about the "sharp end" of curriculum development; namely, about what goes on, to use the now familiar cliché, at the chalkface. We need to know more about the effectiveness of different teaching strategies (for example, video vs. traditional chalk-and-talk, teaching in mother tongue or in language immersion situations). More needs to be done on the value of geography as a vehicle for teaching skills in other areas, such as those of numeracy or the use of language.

C.   Studies Related to the Interface between Science and Didactics

Finally, attention must be given to the important area concerned with the relationship between geography as science and geography as didactic. It was said at the outset, almost by way of a statement of faith, that there has to be some kind of relationship between university and school geography. The reasons for making this assertion are worth spelling out in a little detail. First, although the nature of academic disciplines owes something to their historical development, as scholars such as Hirst[35] and Phenix[36] maintain they nonetheless have a claim to independent existence by virtue of the fact that each represents a coherent way of looking at one aspect of human experience by a mode of enquiry and a frame of reference which is, by and large, agreed upon by practitioners. Whether geography is a "field" or a "form" of knowledge may be beside the point[37] which is that, if it is indeed worthwhile to study people and environment in a framework which is both global and spatial, then that study is, by definition, ge-

---

[35]   P. H. Hirst, "Liberal Education and the nature of knowledge", in R. D. Archambault (ed.)., *Philosophical Analysis and Education* (London: Routledge and Kegan Paul), 1965, 113-138.

[36]   P. H. Phenix, *Realms of Meaning* (London: McGraw Hill, 1964).

[37]   N. J. Graves, *Geography in Education* (London: Heinemann, 1975, 70-71.

ography, whether conducted as a research or a didactic activity. Thus school teachers *should* be able to look to pure geographical research as a source of both substantial knowledge and methodology.

The research problem for geographical educators is to find means of translating, or in the terminology of the Utrecht school referred to above, of "processing" the output of geography as science so that it has pedagogical value. When geographical research is concerned with essentially empirical enquiries within a specified regional frame, this process presents few problems since it is largely a matter of selecting and if necessary editing source materials which enable pupils to recapitulate the investigative procedures of the original researcher. However, when the major emphasis has been, as it frequently has in recent time, upon the investigation of models *per se* then other problems of both a philosophical and practical nature arise.

During the sixties, geography elaborated the links between what have been called synthetic statements, or those whose validation requires empirical observation, and analytic statements, such as in mathematics or formal logic, which have a truth arising from the definition of the terms in which they are stated. Geography moved across the spectrum from being a largely 'factual' science depending on synthetic statements to being one which is at least in part a 'formal' science, depending on analytic statements. It would be inappropriate here to discuss this movement in detail as it has been discussed by Harvey[38], Gregory[39] and many others. However its relevance for geography as didactics lies in the suggestion that an appropriate research task might be to develop what could be called touchstones of pedagogical relevance.

A review which the writer conducted recently of British General Certificate of Education examinations at the Advanced level showed a depressing number of questions on urban geography concerned with the pure geometry of Central Place Systems. It might be argued of course, that such questions test the pupil's capacity for logical and ordered thought, to which the rejoinder would be that these capacities may be tested more efficiently by questions in, say, pure mathematics examinations. Manipulating K-3, K-4, and K-7 networks may be an interesting intellectual game, but it does not seem to have much to do with understanding the way in which real systems of cities and towns work, which should surely be the prime focus of geographical enquiry.

It is in situations such as this that research in geographical didactics can play a role. It was suggested earlier in this paper that reserach in geographical didactics is motivated, not by curiosity about place and space, but by curiosity about how information about place and space is learned. In selecting either substantive content in methodology from academic geography, the critical question is, "*What is its*

---

[38] D. HARVEY, *Explanation in Geography* (London: Edward Arnold, 1969).
[39] D. GREGORY, *op. cit.*

pedagogical value?'' It may be that, in some cases the answer lies in the suitability of a particular activity for developing intellectual skills. In others, a particular body of geographical information or analytical skills may convey something worth knowing about society and how it works, or it may, as in the welfare approaches to geography[40], be a vehicle for social critique. In yet others, geography may be a means of assisting the pupil to find out more about him/herself, and through this, about the human species. In all cases, the criterion is teachability and pedagogical value.

[40] D. M. SMITH, *Human Geography: A Welfare Approach* (London: St. Martin, 1977).

Achevé d'imprimer à Montmagny
par les Travailleurs des ateliers Marquis Ltée
en décembre 1980